GUIDE TO
WEATHER

ROSS REYNOLDS

Precipitation

Condensation

Water vapour
transport

Evaporation

EDITORIAL: *Joanna Potts, Caroline Rayner, Simon Roberts, Kara Turner, Laura Walker*
DESIGN: *Chris Bell, Caroline Ohara, Steve Scanlan,*
PRODUCTION: *Sally Banner*

First published in 2000 by Philip's,
a division of Octopus Publishing Group Ltd,
2–4 Heron Quays, London E14 4JP

Copyright © 2000–2004 Philip's
Revised reprint 2004

ISBN-13 978-0-540-08704-4
ISBN-10 0-540-08704-1

A CIP catalogue record for this book is available
from the British Library.

Printed in China

FRONT COVER : *tl* shallow cumulus, *Telegraph Colour Library*;
tc depression tracks © Philip's; *tr* rainbow, M.V. Young; *b*
weather forecast model © Philip's
BACK COVER : *bl* Reversal of stratospheric winds, winter; *bl*
summer, © Philip's;
THIS PAGE (from top to bottom) : California coast, Tony
Stone; occluded front, Dundee/*NOAA*

Other titles from Philip's

Philip's publish a range of titles
of geographical interest in the same
format as this book, including:

Philip's Minerals, Rocks and Fossils
Philip's Guide to Gems
Philip's Guide to Fossils
Philip's Guide to Global Hazards
Philip's Guide to the Oceans
Philip's Guide to Seashells of the World
Philip's Guide to the State of the World

For details of Philip's products

website
www.philips-maps.co.uk

email
philips@philips-maps.co.uk

tel **020 7644 6940**

fax **020 7644 6986**

Contents

INTRODUCTION

The weather influences all of us either directly or indirectly. In rare circumstances it can threaten our lives with hazardous weather including gales, thick fog, flood-producing rain, lightning and more. Since most of us live and work in urban areas and travel by modern private or public transport, we are less aware of, and less affected by, the weather than we would have been decades ago.

I well remember my primary school teacher saying that the weather is an Englishman's (or anyone's) standby, meaning that it was always a useful medium for striking up a conversation with a stranger. That was in the late 1950s. Since then, especially during the last decade or so, scientists have made us all aware of changes in our atmosphere that are potentially of great consequence to our lives. Nowadays, just about all

of us are at least conscious of predicted future changes in our atmosphere that are linked to the way we live.

The science of the weather has advanced dramatically over recent decades. Today, many national weather agencies can predict weather many days ahead, for the whole world. One major centre, the European Centre for Medium-Range Weather Forecasts (ECMWF) in Reading, UK, is sponsored by over 20 European weather services to forecast the weather for the entire world out to ten days ahead. The continual improvement in weather forecasting is related to better observational networks, faster and better computers, and increased knowledge and understanding of how the atmosphere 'works', including its interaction with the land and ocean surfaces.

Nowadays there is also great international concern about global change and how it will impact upon our everyday lives. The discovery of the Antarctic ozone 'hole' stimulated rapid intergovernmental co-operation to tackle the main causes of the problem. The seasonal ozone hole continues to occur and it is estimated that it is likey to do so until the middle of this century at least.

Global change is principally related to the observed warming of the lower atmosphere in recent decades. Scientists are able to predict future climate change by using computer models. They look at changes over decades – so that we can gain the best possible idea of what temperature and rainfall levels will be like globally, by the year 2050 for example. Work continues to improve these models and to compare them. They form the basis for concerted international effort through responsible governmental planning. That said, the Kyoto Protocol, which sets out the reduction in the emission of greenhouse gases by a certain target period and was signed by virtually all the world's nations in 1992, has yet to be ratified by a sufficient number to give it force in international law. As a result, the outlook for many island states is gloomy, their very existence seriously threatened by the measured and predicted increase in sea-level that is being forced by warming oceans and melting ice. Rising seas are likely to remain a significant problem for decades to come.

Today's scientific methods of prediction haven't always been with us of course. For thousands of years humans have followed signs in the sky that would help to indicate how weather may progress during a day. Some would also have been aware of other natural guides to the possible character of an incoming season, for example the state of berries on a particular shrub or the timing of the migration of birds.

Today we are aware of weather 'lore', sayings that encapsulate such observational skill developed over long periods of time. "Red sky at night, shepherd's delight; red sky at morning, shepherd's warning" is one such saying still in circulation. The "red sky at night" rule works some of the

◀ **Hurricane Ivan**
swirling in the tropical Atlantic Ocean on September 5, 2004. The MODIS instrument aboard NASA's Terra satellite captured this true-colour image of Hurricane Ivan. Modern forecasting tools such as weather satellites, radar and computer models are now able to make reasonable predictions as to when and where a weather event such as Hurricane Ivan might occur.

time but only in regions where the weather systems arrive from the west, even so, the rule is obviously less reliable than today's computer predictions. The number and type of weather sayings in circulation globally is enormous. Some sayings are centuries-old seasonal indicators such as "If snow remains on the trees in November, they will bring out but few buds in the spring" (Germany) or "When birds and badgers are fat in October, expect a cold winter" (USA). Others are short-term, like "If the rain falls on the dew, it will fall all day" (Italy) or "If the wind is northeast three days without rain, eight days will pass before south wind again" (UK).

Another tradition relates to changes in seaweed and pinecones, suggesting that changes in the bulk or shape of seaweed or pinecones indicate the likelihood of rain. It is based on the response of plant life to variations in relative humidity. When this increases with the approach of frontal rain, seaweed and pine cones will absorb some of the moisture, changing their appearance. Seaweed becomes more plump or less dry, and pine cones will partly close. Such humidity-related changes may simply reflect the daily variation in relative humidity under settled conditions, which occurs as the air temperature increases to a peak in the afternoon then decreases to a minimum during the night. True, there will be changes on the approach of moister air ahead of a depression, but for the vast majority of us, the sky is a far more reliable source of harbingers of a frontal system.

The notion that the weather on a particular day of the year may indicate the nature of the weather to come over the following month, or more, is the basis of Groundhog Day in the USA, and St Swithun's Day in the UK.

Groundhog Day, on February 2, takes place at Punxsutawney, Pennsylvania, involving a captive groundhog known as Punxsutawney Phil. If he sees his shadow when he pokes his head out of his burrow, winter will last another six weeks; if he does not see it, spring is just around the corner. If the day is sunny and, therefore, probably cold and anticyclonic, local folklore has it that these conditions will persist. If there is no shadow, it is obviously cloudy and probably milder. However, there is no real evidence that this particular day is the key to forecasting long-term weather patterns.

St Swithun's Day on July 15 in the UK is another example. Swithun died in 862, when he was bishop of Winchester, and he was buried at his own request in the cathedral grounds. After his canonization the following century, it was decided to move his remains to the choir of the cathedral on 15 July. The plan was abandoned, however, after 40 days of rain that began on that day. Lore has it the weather on St Swithun's day is supposed to dictate the nature of the weather for the next 40 days. If it rains on July 15, it will rain for 40 days, if it remains dry, there will be no rain for 40 days. In the cold light of scientific reality, a wet St Swithun's Day is extremely unlikely

▲ *"Red sky at night,*
shepherd's delight, red
sky at morning,
shepherd's warning" is
an example of an old
weather saying that is
still in use today. The
rule works some of the
time, but only where the
weather arrives from
the west.

to start a run of wet weather lasting nearly six weeks in Winchester or anywhere else.

In addition to looking at how forecasts are made today, this book provides an overview of meteorology for those who want to gain a basic understanding of what makes the weather 'tick', and to appreciate what lies behind some of today's great atmospheric environmental issues. If you are interested, for example, in being more involved in taking your own observations, obtaining advice about using weather science in schools, linking up with others interested in the atmospheric environment or receiving magazines and newsletters, there are learned societies you can contact, all with regional centres. All welcome foreign members too.

In Europe, the European Meteorological Society encourages anyone interested in weather and climate to join one of its member societies, for example the UK's Royal Meteorlogical Society. Similar societies exist in the USA, Australia, New Zealand and Canada. They can be contacted by post or via the Web. In addition, the 'Climatological Observers' Link' exists to promote the collection and exchange of weather observations by anyone interested to do so. Useful addresses and websites are listed at the end of the book.

Before looking at the weather in detail, it is necessary to set the scene by explaining some basic facts about the atmosphere's chemical make-up, its structure and layering, and what drives it to stir on a global scale. The large-scale circulation of the oceans also influences the world's weather systems.

The average change in temperature from the surface of the Earth up through the atmosphere is generated from vast numbers of thermal observations taken by meteorologists across all latitudes and through the depth of the atmosphere. This summary of an immense data set is the basis for the definition of the layers of the Earth's atmosphere.

Observations of the weather taken at sites scattered across the Earth's surface and up through the atmosphere provide the information essential for producing an accurate global picture of its patterns. Measurements taken throughout the year enable meteorologists to study the nature and extent of the major seasonal changes that occur in these patterns, both at the surface and at different levels within the atmosphere.

▶ *Average thermal profile* of the atmosphere.

▼ *Zonal mean* is the average of all the separate values within a latitude band.

▼▼ *Average summer* (left) and winter (right) northern hemisphere westerly (positive)/easterly (negative) wind speed (m/sec)

MAKE-UP OF THE ATMOSPHERE

The primitive atmosphere of the Earth may have been produced by gases escaping from within the planet as it was warmed by such processes as radioactive decay. Since that time, the composition of the air has changed dramatically, partly due to the evolution of life. More recently, industrialized human society has had a major impact on the make-up of the atmosphere, the potential consequences of which are attracting a great deal of attention today (*see* pages 130–147).

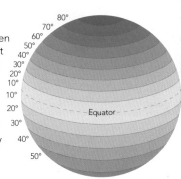

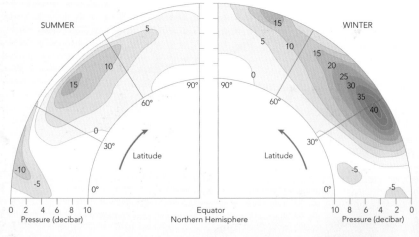

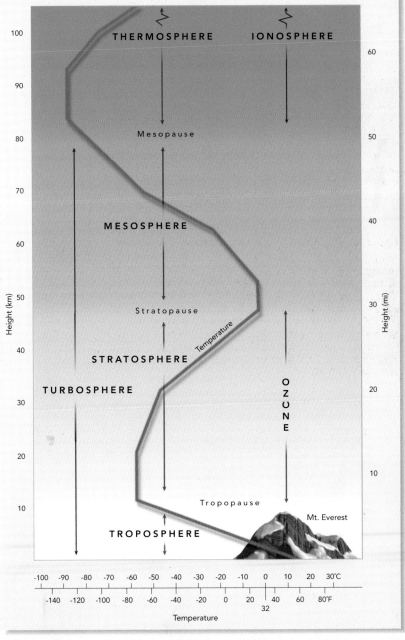

Dry air

The gases that comprise the 'dry' atmosphere occur in fixed proportions up to about 100 km (62 mi) above sea level. This well-mixed layer is known as the **turbosphere**, and within it the mixing is carried out by large-scale weather systems and much smaller-scale turbulence. This region is capped by the **turbopause**, above which lies the **thermosphere**. Here the atmosphere is characterized by layers composed of individual gases separated out according to their molecular weight, shown in the table on page 17. The heavier gases occur at the lower levels of the upper atmosphere.

'Dry' air refers to the gaseous constituents of the Earth's atmosphere – with the exception of water vapour. This is not included because, unlike the gases that occur in fixed amounts, water vapour is highly variable in concentration.

Water vapour resides at lower levels, mainly within the first few kilometres of the atmosphere, because it originates at the Earth's surface. In addition to its gaseous constituents, the air within the lower levels of the atmosphere (the troposphere) contains solid and liquid water in the form of ice, water droplets, clouds and precipitation. Very small particles, known as aerosol, also occur in the same layer; they comprise a suspension of solid and liquid particles with very low settling velocities and their diameters range from about 1/10,000,000,000 of a metre to 1/100,000 of a metre.

Pressure

Pressure is related to the weight of the air above the point at which the measurement is taken. This means that it must be highest at the Earth's surface and decrease continually upwards through the atmosphere until a tenuous ill-defined edge is reached at its outer limit.

AIR DENSITY AND PRESSURE

Site	Height (amsl*) (m)	Air density (kg/m3)	Pressure (mbar)
Mean-sea-level	0	1.23	1,013.2
Telecom Tower, London, UK	189	1.20	990.0
Sky Tower Auckland, New Zealand	328	1.18	970.0
Empire State Building, New York, USA	448	1.17	960.0
Petronas Towers, Kuala Lumpur, Malaysia	452	1.17	958.0
Ben Nevis, UK	1,343	1.07	860.0
Mount Kosciuszko, Australia	2,280	0.95	780.0
Mont Blanc, France	4,810	0.75	550.0
Mount McKinley (Denali), USA	6,194	0.65	460.0
Mount Everest, Nepal	8,848	0.48	315.0
Cruising 747 'jumbo' jet	11,000	0.36	225.0

amsl = above mean-sea-level

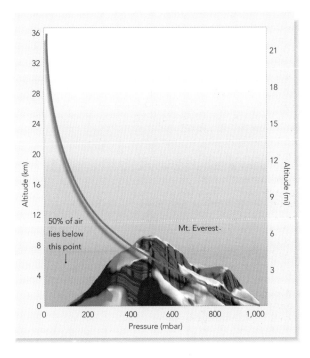

◀ **Atmospheric pressure change** with height. The air thins as the pressure decreases, which is why climbers need oxygen masks to climb peaks such as Mount Everest, in the Himalayas.

The air is compressed under its own weight, so its density also decreases with height. The link between the air's density, pressure and elevation above sea level is summarized in the table on page 10, which uses prominent natural and man-made features as examples.

The annual global mean-sea-level pressure is 1013.2 mbar, which relates to an air density of 1.23 kg/m³. At the top of the Empire State Building in New York, USA, it is typically 53 mbar lower than at sea level; air at the harbourside in New York is about 3% denser than the air at the top of the Empire State Building.

Going up through the highest peaks in Australia, Western Europe, North America and the rest of the world leads to thinner and thinner air, down to a density of 0.48 kg/m³ at the top of Mount Everest, where the average pressure is 315 mbar.

Commercial jets normally use cabin pressures between about 850 and 800 mbar, which is about the same as being in the open air between 1,500 and 2,000 m (4,900 and 6,600 ft) above sea level. Such jets cruise at a level where the outside pressure is around 250 to 200 mbar because that is where they are most fuel-efficient. Lowering the cabin pressure to a tolerable value means that the smaller difference between it and the outside air decreases stress on the jet's fuselage. The cabin pressure is lowered gradually as an aircraft climbs after take-off and is gradually increased during descent into landing.

THE TROPOSPHERE

The troposphere is the lowest layer of the atmosphere. The term 'troposphere' was coined by Léon Teisserenc de Bort (1855–1913), a French meteorologist and one of the first pioneers in the use of balloons for taking temperature 'soundings' of the atmosphere. This layer is characterized by temperatures that, on average, decrease with height, and by the presence of almost all the atmosphere's clouds and weather. Something like 80% of the mass of the atmosphere is contained in the troposphere, along with virtually all the clouds, water vapour and precipitation.

The prefix 'tropos' is Greek for 'turn', and it was used in the name because the layer is generally well mixed by vertical circulations of the air, which vary in depth and vigour. Ascent of an air particle from low level to the vicinity of the tropopause can occur in a few minutes in the most vigorous thundercloud updraughts, while in clear conditions the journey may take several days. This type of air motion is a hallmark of the troposphere, although it does not occur everywhere all of the time.

The heating at the Earth's surface, at the base of the troposphere, may be likened to heating a pan of soup or some fluid on the burner of a stove, when heat is partly transferred up through the fluid by convection. In the case of the atmosphere, this happens as thermals or as 'bubbling' cumulus clouds.

Because the depth of the overturning motions is related to the intensity of surface heating, on average the layer is deepest in the tropics and becomes shallower towards the poles. There is a seasonal variation outside the lowest latitudes such that the troposphere is deepest in summertime.

When air ascends, it cools at a rate that depends on whether it is 'dry' (i.e. without clouds) or 'saturated' (cloudy). Conversely, air that descends will warm at the same rate as ascending air, depending on

▶ *Average wintertime depth* of the troposphere in relation to the location of the major westerly jetstreams and surface pressure centres.

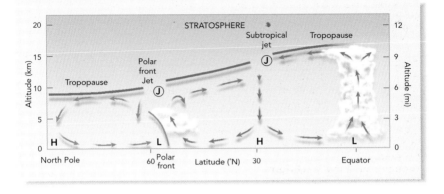

whether the sinking happens within clear skies or within a cloud. Ascending air moves into steadily reducing pressure, which causes it first to expand and then consequently cool. Descending air is compressed as it subsides gradually into higher pressure and thus is warmed. So the up-and-down motions that typify the troposphere are associated with cooler air aloft and warmer air below.

Lapse rates

The average lapse rate of temperature – the rate at which it falls with height – is almost 6°C/km (3°F/1,000 ft), but values can vary greatly with time and space.

The ascent of bubbles or layers of air leads to cooling associated with their gradual expansion – this is termed adiabatic expansion or cooling. It means that, for example, as a 'bubble' expands when it rises, its internal energy – or the rate

▼The ascent and descent of a dry air bubble in the troposphere at the dry adiabatic lapse rate. The dry air bubble (cloudless) expands as it rises, causing it to cool.

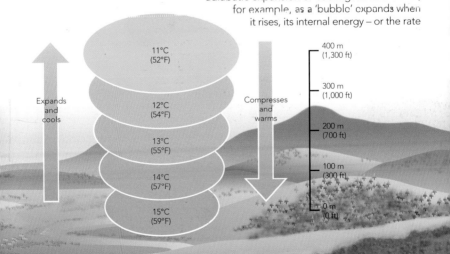

13

at which its molecules whizz around – decreases. This leads to a drop in its temperature. If the bubble is cloudless, it will cool at a fixed rate, known as the dry adiabatic lapse rate (DALR), which is 9.8°C/km (5.5°F/1,000 ft).

Conversely, when air sinks towards the surface, it will be compressed and warmed at this rate. If ascending air is damp enough to produce cloud droplets, latent heat will be released, which warms the air and offsets the DALR. This reduced rate of cooling is called the saturated adiabatic lapse rate (SALR), and it varies according to the quantity of water vapour contained in the air. It is the rate of temperature decrease that would be measured within a cloud.

Other processes can also affect the air's temperature, such as radiative warming and cooling. In this case, gas molecules absorb solar radiation and are warmed by it, then cool by radiating heat away in all directions.

THE STRATOSPHERE

The stratosphere was discovered independently by two European scientists in 1902. Richard Assmann and Léon Teisserenc de Bort both established that above about 10 km (6 mi) the air temperature either remains constant with height or actually increases; it was de Bort who first applied the term 'stratosphere' to this layer. This layer extends from the tropopause up to 50 km (31 mi) above sea level, where its maximum temperature is reached. As an annual average above middle latitudes, this is about 0°C (32°F).

This layer is distinctly different from the constantly churning troposphere below it. Its very name indicates that it is stratified, or layered, since it is a region within which temperature is constant or increases with height. It is colder below and warmer above, and this suggests that the overturning motions in the stratosphere are reduced in contrast to those in the troposphere (which is warmer below and colder above).

Sometimes, extremely vigorous, and thus very deep, cumulonimbus clouds (see pages 66–71) formed within the troposphere – in the tropics or over the interior of the USA in summer, for example – can actually overshoot into the lower reaches of the stratosphere. It is so stable and so dry in this region, however, that the upward-shooting cloud is soon evaporated by mixing with the ambient air.

▼ *The reversal of polar stratospheric* winds from winter (top) to summer (bottom). The wind changes are caused by the drop in temperature, during the extended polar night in winter and rise in temperature, during the extended day in summer.

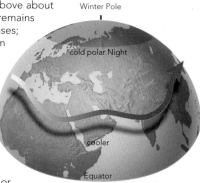

Winter Pole

cold polar Night

cooler

Equator

Summer Pole

warmer polar day

cold

Equator

Ozone

Increased temperature in the middle and upper stratosphere is caused by the absorption of short-wave solar radiation by ozone, a form of oxygen molecule that has three atoms rather than the much more common two-atom form of the gas (see page 137). The existence of ozone at these levels is due to the splitting, or dissociation, of oxygen molecules into two oxygen atoms by the action of that same short-wave radiation.

This means that ozone is constantly being created and destroyed by natural processes in the stratosphere, mainly at a height of 20–30 km (12–19 mi). This has been happening for millions of years and has established a natural balance of the gas in the lower to middle stratosphere.

The complex chemical reactions that occur within the ozone layer mean that some 90% of the potentially harmful ultraviolet radiation that streams into the atmosphere in the solar beam is absorbed. Today, the artificial destruction of ozone is of enormous concern internationally, since such depletion will lead to the increased risk of harmful ultraviolet radiation reaching the Earth's surface (see pages 137–146).

Polar day and night

In the polar stratosphere there is a marked seasonal change in the air temperature, which is caused mainly by the prolonged months of darkness during the polar night and the similarly extended period of light during the polar day. This means that at stratospheric levels, the polar region is colder than lower latitudes in the winter, but warmer in the summer. This seasonal flip in the temperature gradient between the pole and the lower latitudes is associated with a change in the wind circulation at these levels. Thus during the depth of the polar night, there are strong westerlies, while during the height of the polar summer, the circulation is weaker and easterly.

THE MESOSPHERE

The 'meso', or middle, region lies above the stratopause and impinges on the lower ionosphere. It is characterized by temperature that decreases with increasing height, from something like 0°C (32°F) at its base to around –90°C (–130°F) at the mesopause, where the atmospheric pressure is about 1/100,000 of the sea-level value.

Mother-of-pearl clouds

Although the stratosphere is dry, on rare occasions clouds may form within it. These are termed nacreous, or 'mother-of-pearl', clouds. They are believed to be made of ice crystals, and form at the smooth crests of vertical wave motions within the lower and middle stratosphere. Typically, nacreous clouds occur up to about 30 km (19 mi), are lenticular (lens-like) in form and exhibit a very fine, delicate structure. They are usually stationary, which suggests that they are produced by some kind of physical feature such as mountains. They also often display brilliant iridescence. This occurs as tinted areas that are most often red and green, but occasionally blue and green; these are caused by the diffraction of sunlight by very small cloud particles. Nacreous clouds are not significant in terms of weather, but they play a crucial role in the formation of the Antarctic ozone 'hole' (see page 141).

This profile, which is similar in pattern to the troposphere, promotes vertical circulations that occasionally lead to cloud formation over polar regions in the summertime. Typically, the cloud occurs at elevations of 80–85 km (50–53 mi) and can be viewed with the naked eye only around twilight against a dark sky, when the troposphere is mainly cloud-free. Because this cloud is high enough to be illuminated when the surface of the Earth is shrouded in darkness, it is called noctilucent. Most commonly, it may be observed polewards of 50 degrees latitude, around the midnight hours during summer.

▲ *Noctilucent cloud over Yorkshire, UK. Also known as polar mesospheric clouds, they are generally observed in higher latitude countries at twilight.*

THE THERMOSPHERE

This deep layer stretches from the mesopause to the outer limit of the Earth's atmosphere; it lies above the well-mixed turbosphere (also known as the homosphere) and is sometimes termed the heterosphere. The thermosphere is characterized by increasing temperature with elevation, such that at heights between 300 and 500 km (190–310 mi), it reaches between 500°C (930°F) and 2,000°C (3,600°F). This temperature range is directly attributable to solar activity, the highest values associated with an active Sun. It is within the thermosphere that the gases separate out according to their molecular weights (see table, top right).

▶ *Solar and terrestrial radiation emission spectra. Because the Sun is extremely hot it emits more energy, but in shorter wavelengths. The Earth emits very little energy in comparison and in longer wavelengths.*

The Sun, radiation and the atmosphere

The virtually ceaseless motion of the Earth's atmosphere and oceans, both on global and very local scales, is ultimately related to the massive and endless stream of energy leaving the Sun. The Solar Constant – the energy available in the solar beam at the outer limit of the atmosphere – is 1.38 kW/m^2 at right angles to the beam. This energy is transferred through space by the process of radiation. Unlike other forms of heat transfer, such as convection and conduction, this does not require a physical medium to be effective.

COMPONENTS OF THE THERMOSPHERE		
Component (Gas)	Molecular weight	Fraction of total molecules
Krypton	83.70	1 part per million
Ozone	48.00	0 to 12 parts per million
Carbon dioxide	44.01	340 parts per million
Argon	39.94	0.0093
Oxygen	32.00	0.2095
Nitrogen	28.02	0.7808
Neon	20.18	18 parts per million
Water vapour	18.02	0 to 0.04
Helium	4.00	5 parts per million
Hydrogen	2.02	0.5 parts per million

The radiative energy emitted by anything depends on its temperature. The hotter a body, the more energy it will emit, and it will do so at shorter wavelengths (the wavelength is the distance between two adjacent crests in the wave pattern that characterizes radiation). This measurement is the means by which the radiation is defined across a wide electromagnetic spectrum, from the extremely short ultraviolet to the very long waves that are used to for radio broadcasts.

A body such as the Sun, with a surface temperature of about 6,000K (Kelvin: 0°C is equivalent to 273K, 0°F is equivalent to 255K) has an emission curve that peaks at short wavelengths. The Earth, with a mean atmospheric

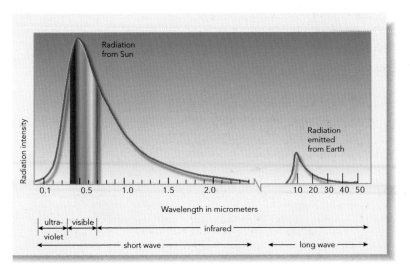

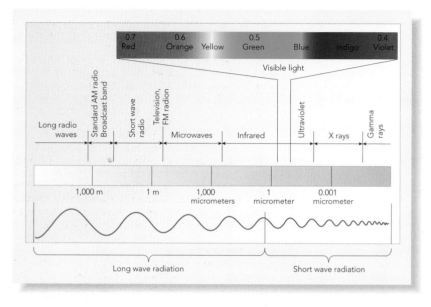

0.7 Red
0.6 Orange Yellow
0.5 Green
Blue Indigo
0.4 Violet

Visible light

Standard AM radio Broadcast band

Short wave radio

Television, FM radion

Long radio waves

Microwaves

Infrared

Ultraviolet

X rays

Gamma rays

1,000 m — 1 m — 1,000 micrometers — 1 micrometer — 0.001 micrometer

Long wave radiation

Short wave radiation

◀ *Apollo 13* photograph, 1970.
▼ *The elctromagnetic spectrum* with 'classes' of radiation.

▲ *Varying path length* and incidence angle of the solar beam in southern hemisphere summer.

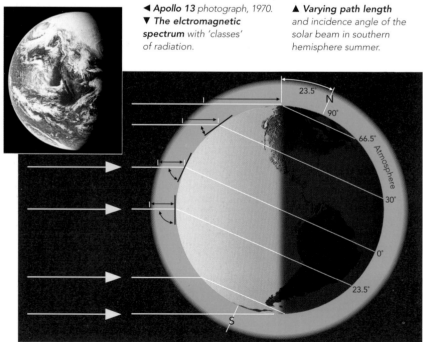

23.5°
N
90°
66.5°
Atmosphere
30°
0°
23.5°
S

temperature of about 255K, emits very little in comparison, and the emission is at longer wavelengths. However, this terrestrial radiation is crucially important in the heat budget of the planet's surface and atmosphere.

In an average year, the amount of solar energy absorbed by the Earth's surface and atmosphere varies markedly from equator to pole. There is little variation within the tropics, where about 300W/m^2 flows in, while in polar areas, it falls to below 100W/m^2. This pattern is dictated partly by the angle of incidence of the incoming sunshine (solar radiation) and the thickness of the atmosphere through which it must travel. Low sun elevation and long atmospheric path length for the sunshine combine in higher latitudes to produce small values. In contrast to this steep solar curve, the Earth and its atmosphere emit their terrestrial radiation to space so that, although more is being emitted in the warmest, tropical, zone, the energy falls off gently towards the poles. In this case, emission ranges from about 260 to 120/180 W/m^2.

Surplus and deficit

The two curves (below) point to the presence of a region of the Earth that, on this annual average basis, receives more solar radiation input than it loses in terrestrial output. This surplus occurs between about 35 degrees north and 35 degrees south. Conversely, the regions in each hemisphere outside these subtropical latitudes experience a radiative deficit where more energy is lost to space than is gained from the Sun.

These patterns pose a problem. Why does it not become progressively hotter in the tropics as the years go by, and colder in the 'extratropics'? If there were no atmosphere or oceans, and if the Earth were simply a ball of rock, the

▶ **Annual average incoming solar** and outgoing terrestrial radiation. The region of the Earth represented by the red shaded area between the two curves, receives more solar radiation than it loses from the Earth. This creates a surplus of radiation. The blue regions lose more radiation than they receive.

ANNUAL RADIATION BUDGET

Incoming radiation

Outgoing radiation

Surplus

Energy (Watts per square metre)

Equator

Deficit

Deficit

LATITUDE (DEGREES)

Southern Hemisphere   Northern Hemisphere

tropics would become progressively hotter, to such an extent that the outgoing Earth radiation would balance the incoming flow from the Sun. Similarly, the extratropics would become colder and colder until the Earth's outgoing energy fell sufficiently to balance the supply from the Sun.

In reality, the difference between the surplus and deficit at low and high latitudes forces the atmosphere and ocean into carrying some of the excess heat from the tropics to the deficit zone outside, acting like massive convectors. This word is appropriate, because the heat is transported in the same manner that a convection heater warms a room by heating the air (fluid), which then circulates around the room as a warm current. In this case, both the atmosphere and the ocean act as global fluids, constantly ameliorating conditions in both regions – they keep the tropics cooler than they otherwise would be and warm the extratropics above a significantly colder possibility.

The annual pattern masks large seasonal variation. Although the amount of solar radiation absorbed in the tropics varies little throughout the year, mirrored by the limited seasonality of tropical temperature, the values at higher latitudes vary enormously. The picture for December illustrates the fact that the majority of the northern, winter hemisphere is in deficit, while the summer hemisphere is largely a region of surplus. The principal reason for this is the change from the prolonged polar night and 'dark' mid-latitudes in the winter to the polar day and 'light' mid-latitudes in the summer.

Therefore, the forcing pattern is strongest in the winter, because the difference between the equator and pole is at its greatest; in the summer, it is much weaker.

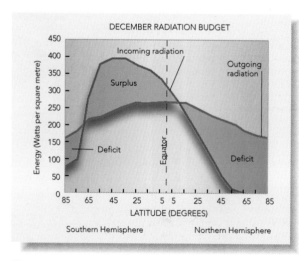

◀ *December average incoming solar* and *outgoing terrestrial radiation. Most of the northern, winter hemisphere has a deficit of radiation; the majority of the southern, summer hemisphere has a surplus of radiation.*

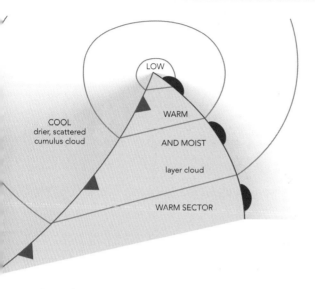

LOW

WARM

AND MOIST

layer cloud

COOL
drier, scattered
cumulus cloud

WARM SECTOR

◄ **Basic contrasts in an open wave** mid-latitude frontal depression. Warm-sectors move towards the pole to be cooled, while the cold front brings cooler weather towards the equator to be warmed.

Working depressions

Broadly, this is the reason why, for example, that the storms that run across western Europe so frequently in the cooler season are much windier than their warmer-season counterparts. Their increased vigour is a sign of the larger amount of heat transport that they undertake.

These depressions, or lows, are very common across mid-latitude western shores – so much so that they are hallmarks of the weather in those areas. They are travelling disturbances that are characterised by extensive cloud, rain and wind and are mostly 'frontal' in nature. This means that they have attendant warm and cold fronts (see pages 56–61) that are, respectively, the forward or leading edges of extensive areas of warm and cold air. Between the two fronts lies the warm sector, which is a region of warm, moist subtropical air that moves bodily towards higher latitudes. Behind the cold front, the cooler, often showery, polar air sweeps generally towards lower latitudes. These mobile lows are nature's way of responding to the global atmosphere's demand to cool off at lower latitudes and warm up in higher latitudes.

WORKING OCEANS

Ocean currents play an important role in influencing the atmosphere, not only globally, but also on regional and local scales. The distance of a location from the sea, its elevation above sea level, its exposure and its latitude all have roles to play in the nature of the weather experienced.

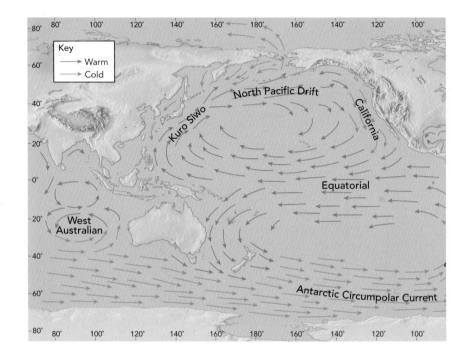

The Gulf Stream, the North Atlantic Drift and the Kuro Siwa are all examples of warm water being exported from the tropical 'boilerhouse' and all three have a significant impact on the climates of distant shores.

The principal warm ocean currents of the southern hemisphere are known as the Brazil and Agulhas Currents. The extensive region of warm water that washes the shores of eastern Australia is also significant.

In contrast, the cool Canaries and the California Currents are parts of the grand design to transport cooler water towards the equator for warming. On their way, they influence the weather along the adjacent coastlines dramatically. They do this because when their cool waters are overrun by relatively warmer and damp air, extensive sea fog or low-level layer cloud is formed as the lower atmosphere is chilled (see page 86). Perhaps the best-known example is the frequent fog and low cloud that occasionally laps across San Francisco's Golden Gate Bridge, USA.

Sea-Surface Circulation

The pattern of large-scale ocean surface currents is more or less a mirror of the average wind patterns at the sea-surface. In other words, the sea-surface circulation is essentially wind-driven, although both warm and cold ocean streams do have an important impact on the weather and climate over the sea and across adjacent land areas.

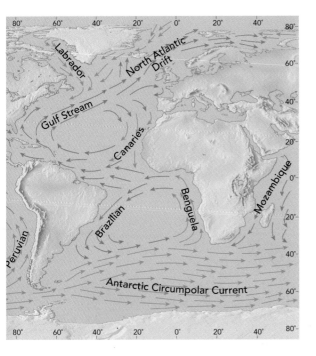

◀ **Major surface ocean currents.** *The currents help to redistribute heat throughout the oceans. The currents influence weather at a global and local scale.*

The western flanks of the southern continents are influenced by cold oceanic flows towards the equator in the form of the Peru (or Humboldt), the Benguela and the West Australian Currents As with the cold California Current, the Humboldt Current is associated with the extensive low cloud and sea fog that occurs along the part of the coasts of Peru and Chile. In comparison to the northern hemisphere's ocean circulation, the southern oceans are markedly cooler, because they are influenced by the cold Antarctic Circumpolar Current at high latitudes.

Averaging one weather station's time series of conditions such as surface temperature, sea-level pressure or wind speed produces a summary of the impact of transient weather features at that particular location. Such arithmetic averaging provides 'mean' values of the measurements. When these values are mapped across the Earth, they reveal the large-scale average patterns of weather phenomena that span weeks, months, seasons or even years.

MEAN-SEA-LEVEL PRESSURE

Averaging the mean-sea-level atmospheric pressure for a number of Januarys and Julys summarizes the mean location and intensity of lows, troughs, highs and ridges during the extreme seasons. Broadly, high pressure areas tend to be associated with dry, settled conditions, whereas low pressure regions relate to the frequent occurrence of cloudy, wet and windy weather.

Northern winter and southern summer

Major features during a typical northern winter and southern summer express the common presence of disturbed and unsettled weather.

The middle-latitude cyclones

The Iceland Low and Aleutian Low, which occur in the higher latitudes of both the North Atlantic and Pacific Oceans respectively, are reflections of the travelling low-pressure systems that run typically from south-west to northeast across these oceans during the winter months. The minimum pressure values mark the point where, on average, the depressions, or cyclones, reach their deepest (lowest).

The southwest/northeast alignment of their troughs indicates the mean track of the depressions in the winter. The map shows that the long-term average value across the centres of the Iceland and Aleutian

Areas of Low Pressure

There is no particular value that makes an area of low pressure 'low'. It is simply a minimum value that occurs over the region of interest. A low could be as little as, perhaps, 930 mbar in a very deep Atlantic depression on a winter's day, or as 'high' as 1,015 mbar, in a summertime 'heat low' over land.

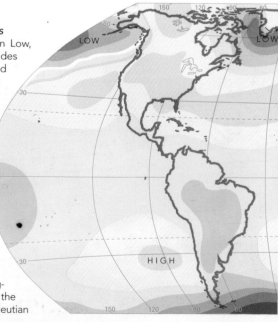

Lows is around 995–1,000 mbar. It also demonstrates the large size of these pressure features, which are typically a few thousand kilometres across.

The trough that stretches northeastwards from the Iceland Low is more extensive than that linked to the Aleutian Low. This is largely an expression of how the travelling cyclones are able to penetrate deeply into the Arctic Basin via the broad Norwegian Sea, in contrast to the more limited poleward excursions across the Bering Strait.

Continental anticyclones

In contrast to the maritime lows in the winter hemisphere, the extensive cold continents are marked mainly by the presence of very large highs, or anticyclones. The centres of

▲ *January mean-sea-level* pressure (mbar). *See key below for pressure measurements.*

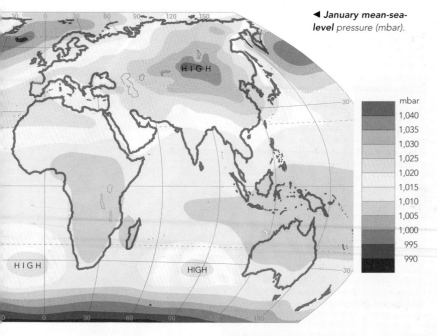

◄ *January mean-sea-level* pressure (mbar).

mbar
1,040
1,035
1,030
1,025
1,020
1,015
1,010
1,005
1,000
995
990

these two major features lie deep in the middle-latitude continental interiors of Asia and North America. The most intense is the Asian High, with a long-term value above 1,040 mbar; the centre over the United States is less intense than the Asian High (about 1,020–1,025 mbar), but, nevertheless, it still has a strong influence on the regional weather.

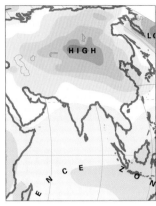

The highs are the products of intense radiative cooling (see pages 84–85) that occurs across these vast land masses in the winter. As with lows, there is no specific value of pressure that defines such a feature as a 'high' – the pressure quoted is simply the maximum value that occurs across an extensive region. Therefore, a high could have a value of, perhaps, 1,055 mbar on a particular day, and 1,015 mbar on another. The important aspect is that it is the largest value observed, with pressure gradually increasing towards it across a few thousand kilometres in a typical anticyclone.

▲ *January mean-sea-level* pressure for North America and Asia. The large, cold continents are categorized by regions of very high pressure, or anticyclones. Both continental anticyclones have strong influence on local weather.

Subtropical oceanic anticyclones

In addition to the cold continental winter anticyclones, regions of high pressure occur across the subtropical North Atlantic and Pacific Oceans. These are the Azores and Hawaiian Highs, which dominate the weather in these regions. They are warmer than their continental counterparts, and deeper, stretching throughout the depth of the troposphere. Cold anticyclones are shallow, recognizable as highs only up to 1.5–2 km (c.1 mi) above the surface.

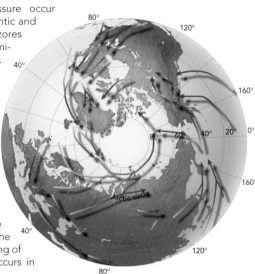

The Equatorial Trough

Moving towards the equator from the subtropical anticyclones reveals a broad area of low-latitude minimum of pressure known as the Equatorial Trough. This is something of a misnomer, since the feature occurs in the south, across the intensely heated southern continents of South America, Southern Africa and Australasia.

The middle-latitude southern ocean is characterized by an elongated circumpolar belt of low pressure, which is virtually unbroken, unlike the northern lows. Its presence is a reflection of depressions that travel unimpeded around the open southern ocean, providing the strong westerly winds associated with the Roaring Forties that skirt the Antarctic continent.

In contrast, the North Atlantic and Pacific storm tracks run much more southwest/northeast, influenced by the alignment of eastern North American and eastern Asian coastlines in the middle latitudes. These depressions feed off the strong thermal contrasts that exist between the continental and oceanic regions in the northern hemisphere: the temperature gradient separating them has the same orientation.

There are warm subtropical anticyclones located over the South Pacific, South Indian and South Atlantic Oceans, which give way northwards to the Equatorial Trough. There are no continental highs because these regions are strongly heated in the summer and are characterized by this shallow low-pressure (1,005–1,010 mbar) feature.

The Polar Regions
Polar regions are subjected to seasonal changes of pressure. The Arctic tends to experience a weak high in the winter and a shallow low in the summer. The relatively high elevations throughout the Antarctic mean that reducing the pressure values to sea level becomes unrealistic. Broadly, it experiences relatively high pressure throughout the year.

The poles are also affected by geography. In the northern hemisphere, the continents widen towards the pole and surround the Arctic Ocean, while in the southern hemisphere, they taper towards the pole, giving way to the circumpolar ocean that surrounds the massive continent of Antarctica. The result of this marked difference is that frontal depressions tend to run due west-east, flanking the Antarctic continent, as noted earlier. In contrast, those of the Northern Hemisphere extratropical oceans most often track from southwest to northeast in association with the thermal gradients that are aligned in the same way, parallel to the orientation of the coastlines there.

The North Atlantic Oscillation (NAO)
This phenomenon is essentially a 'see-saw' in mass exchange between the North Atlantic's Azores High and Iceland Low during the winter season. A positive NAO index occurs when there is a large pressure difference between the Azores and Iceland; such a steep gradient is associated with stronger westerly flow into Europe and generally more vigorous travelling lows. It is linked to milder, wetter than

◄ **Major Northern Hemisphere** depression tracks in January. The tracks are influenced partly by the position of the North American and Asian continents.

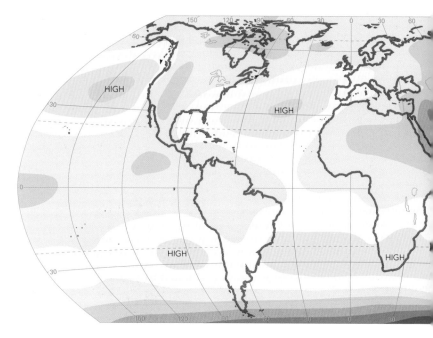

average winters over much of Europe and also to cooler than average conditions across comparable eastern North American latitudes.

In contrast, a negative NAO index means weaker than average flow across the Atlantic towards Europe, and cooler winters across much of that continent. The graph on page 29 illustrates the fluctuating nature of the NAO index over more than a century.

Northern summer and southern winter

The centres of low pressure, so marked over the northern oceans in January, are much weaker or barely discernible in July, having shifted polewards. The extensive continental anticyclones are now replaced by large-scale low-pressure features. Over Asia, this change is marked by a depression centred across western India and Pakistan. The switch over this continent from extensive high to extensive low pressure is linked to the evolution of the monsoon (*see* pages 156–157) from its winter to summer phase.

The summer hemisphere subtropical highs intensify or become higher. Both exhibit an increase of some 5 mbar and migrate a few degrees of latitude northwards. As in winter, the east–west continental/oceanic pattern in this hemisphere is caused by the break-up of the major pressure features into very large highs and lows. The Earth-girdling

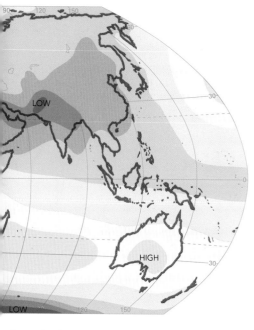

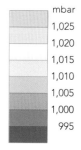

◄ July mean-sea-level pressure (mbar). By July the areas of high pressure have moved towards the Southern Hemisphere for the southern winter. Even during the winter however, the pressure doesn't reach the levels of the northern winter.

mbar
1,025
1,020
1,015
1,010
1,005
1,000
995

Equatorial Trough, over the continents especially, exhibits a substantial seasonal migration towards the equator.

The subtropical anticyclones in the wintertime southern hemisphere form a virtually complete belt, while the circumpolar lows still occur around the Antarctic with noticeably low pressure values.

WIND

The relative locations of the highs and lows in January and July determine the pattern of prevailing winds and thus, in part, the nature of the weather experienced around the Earth.

▼ North Atlantic Oscillation (NAO) index, 1864–2001 (Hurrell). This index represents the difference in the Dec–March average mean-sea-level pressure between Lisbon, Portugal and Reykjavik, Iceland. It shows the strength of the circulation over the winter eastern North Atlantic.

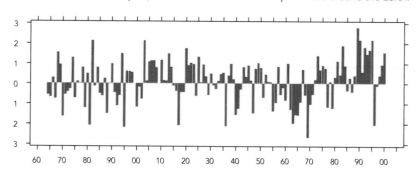

Northern winter and southern summer

In January, the North and South Atlantic, and their surroundings, are influenced by the important source regions of air: the two subtropical anticyclones. At the surface, the winds flow clockwise out of these in the northern hemisphere, and anticlockwise in the southern hemisphere. Parts of these outflows run towards the equator from both highs as the Northeast and Southeast Trades. Together, these culminate in the Intertropical Convergence Zone (ITCZ).

The Trades and the Intertropical Convergence Zone

The Trades are known for their strength and constancy over the tropical oceans, but they slow dramatically as they converge towards each other and enter the

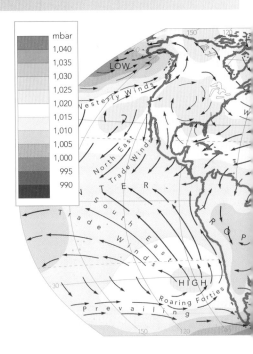

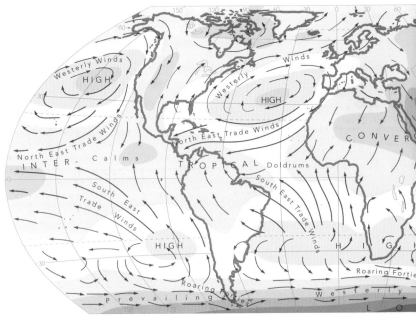

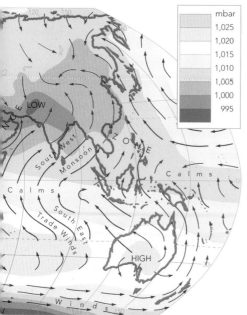

▲ *January mean-sea-level* pressure (mbar) and wind.

◄ *July mean-sea-level* pressure (mbar) and wind. *The locations of the highs and lows in January and July influence global wind patterns.*

ITCZ. This feature, most noticeable over the oceans, is typified by the infamously light and variable winds of the Doldrums. The Trades exist throughout the year, with marked and important migrations north and south of the ITCZ, particularly over the tropical continents.

The ITCZ is also well known for very strong ascent caused by the surface convergence of the hot, humid Trades; this shows up as cloud clusters that produce many thunderstorms. Thus it is a feature of global significance, especially as it supplies water for much of

31

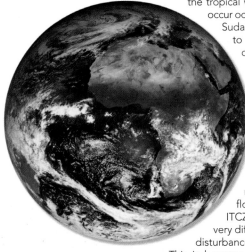

▲ Meteosat visible image *on a January day. The image illustrates a typical southern summer location for the ITCZ.*

the tropical world. The disastrous droughts that occur occasionally across parts of Ethiopia or Sudan can be related to the ITCZ's failure to spread far enough north, or a lack of activity in terms of the deep convective clouds that produce the life-giving downpours.

The Meteosat full-disc visible image (left) illustrates a typical northern winter location for the ITCZ. It stretches around low latitudes and dips farthest south into the heated summertime southern continents, producing a significant seasonal maximum of rainfall. Although the average wind flow for February points to a 'smooth' ITCZ, the day-to-day pattern can be very different, with cloud- and rain-bearing disturbances presenting a complex picture. This is because the monthly averaged flow fields smooth out the great daily variability in the wind pattern.

On the eastern and western flanks of the subtropical anticyclones, the air flows generally parallel to the adjacent coasts but also penetrates into the southern continents to supply the ITCZ.

The middle-latitude westerlies

On the poleward sides of the anticyclones, major warm and moist currents of air move towards the poles as southwesterlies and northwesterlies in the North and South Atlantic respectively. Across the British Isles and western Europe, the southwesterly wind direction predominates. This maritime stream of air contrasts strongly with that on the other side of the North Atlantic, which affects Labrador, the Maritime Provinces and the northeastern USA. Here, the prevailing wind direction is northwesterly, between the Iceland Low and the high over the USA. This means that most often the air comes from the cold, dry regions of North America's higher latitudes.

▼ Mean location of the ITCZ *in February. It represents the average location of where the northeast and southeast trades flow together and also therefore indicates where that month's tropical rainfall maximum occurs.*

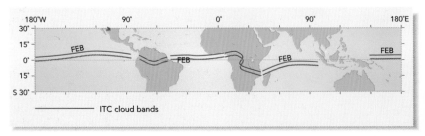

ITC cloud bands

▲ *Thermal infrared image* of an elongated frontal cloud band (centre to top right) and cold air flowing off a springtime USA (top left): the weather is clear on land; but shows showers over the western Atlantic.

In a similar fashion, mild and moist southwesterlies flow towards southern Alaska and western Canada. The situation here differs from that in the northeastern Atlantic because of the Rocky Mountains, which are aligned more or less at right angles to the tracks of the travelling lows. Much of the precipitation from the northeastern Pacific depressions is deposited on the Rockies, to the detriment of the arid high plains to the east. In fact, the dryness of the Plains is related to the presence of the extensive rain-and-snow scavenging mountains to the west (see page 43). On the contrary, Atlantic depressions can move right across the lower land of northern Europe unimpeded.

On the western flank of the Aleutian Low, the predominant flow is from the northwest, from very cold stretches of Russia and northern China.

During the summer in the southern hemisphere, the westerlies blow parallel to the lines of latitude, between the subtropical highs of the South Atlantic, South Indian

▲ *Mean annual precipitation* (cm) over North America.

and South Pacific Oceans and the higher-latitude, low-pressure belt.

Winds in the region of Asia are dominated by flow from the wintertime high into the Aleutian low systems. They either blow into the ITCZ as the Northeast Monsoon, or blow towards the Arctic Ocean. Although the North American High is important, it does not dominate such an extensive region.

Northern summer and southern winter

The Trades and the Intertropical Convergence Zone

The ITCZ reaches its northernmost limit during the height of the northern summer, its most 'famous' excursion being across southern Asia. This seasonal change in the surface winds across India, for example, is the signature of the Monsoon, which takes its name from an Arabic word meaning 'season'. The convergence zone and associated low centre and troughs contrast markedly with the January pattern of extensive northeasterlies across this region.

Similar, but less extensive, seasonal wind reversals also affect the southern part of West Africa, the southwestern USA and northern Mexico.

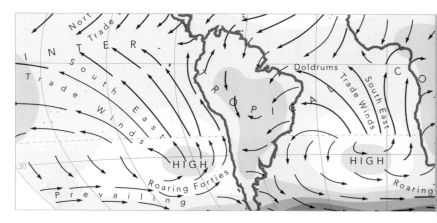

The middle-latitude westerlies

These still occur in the northern ocean basins, but generally are less extensive and less vigorous than in the winter months. The subtropical highs on the westerlies' southern flank intensify into the summer and shift slightly polewards. They still supply the Trades, which, as in January, are most significant across the tropical oceans. The Roaring Forties of the Southern Ocean persist virtually all year, blowing powerfully between the oceanic subtropical highs and the circumpolar low-pressure region.

Continental anticyclones

Apart from Antarctica and Australia, the less extensive continents of the southern hemisphere do not have any substantial highs associated with them. Only Australia is large enough in the subtropical/middle latitudes to produce an anticyclone and, thus, to influence the mean wind pattern regionally.

▲ *Meteosat visible image on an August day. The ITCZ's northern summer location over Africa is clear to see.*

▼ *January mean-sea-level pressure (mbar) and wind. The heated summer continents are characterized by low pressure in contrast to the three oceanic highs.*

Vertical wind patterns

So far, the winds under consideration have been those blowing across the Earth's surface. The flow from surface highs into surface lows implies that there must be some connection through large-scale vertical movements of air.

By considering the average wind flow patterns at various horizontal levels within the troposphere, meteorologists are able to deduce the associated pattern of vertical motion that connects a high with a low. The result illustrates the strong

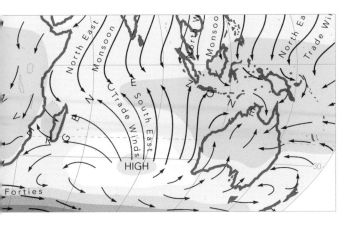

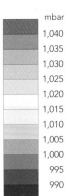

mbar
1,040
1,035
1,030
1,025
1,020
1,015
1,010
1,005
1,000
995
990

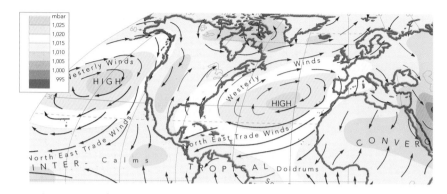

ascent linked to the very extensive swirling of air as it enters a surface low, and the deep descent that supplies the air blowing out of a surface high.

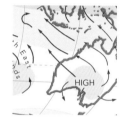

Hadley cell

Each hemisphere displays three distinct types of vertical air circulation, known as cells. The deepest, most powerful and most extensive is the Hadley, or tropical, cell, named after the English scientist George Hadley, who suggested its existence in the first half of the 18th century. It comprises:

1. Generally very vigorous, tropical thunderstorms (known as 'hot towers') associated with the low-level convergence

▲ *July mean-sea-level pressure* (mbar) and wind. Australia is the only southern continent large enough to produce a wintertime anticyclone.

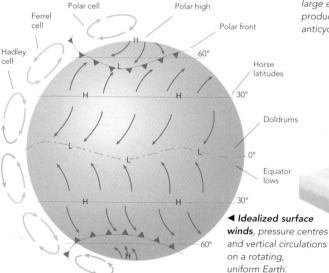

◄ *Idealized surface winds,* pressure centres and vertical circulations on a rotating, uniform Earth.

of warm, moisture-laden air in the ITCZ. This is a very significant region of heavy precipitation that supplies many tropical locations with life-giving seasonal rains.

2. Flow from the top of this thundery zone, in the upper troposphere, towards both poles. This air gradually cools as it moves polewards and, at around 30°N and 30°S, sinks through the troposphere. This region of deep subsidence is linked to the subtropical highs and generally very dry weather. It is no coincidence that most of the world's hot deserts occur beneath this region of persistently subsiding air.

3. Surface return flow from subtropical highs towards the ITCZ as the Northeast and Southeast Trade Winds. These strong winds pick up vast amounts of water vapour by evaporation from the warm tropical oceans over which they flow. This increasingly humid air converges from each flank into the ITCZ, where there is vigorous ascent within the massive thunderstorms that characterize the zone. Therefore, most of the rain that falls from these cumulonimbus clouds comes from evaporation over the tropical oceans.

Ferrel cell

Much weaker than the Hadley cell, the Ferrel, or middle latitude, cell is named after the 19th-century American meteorologist William Ferrel. It comprises:

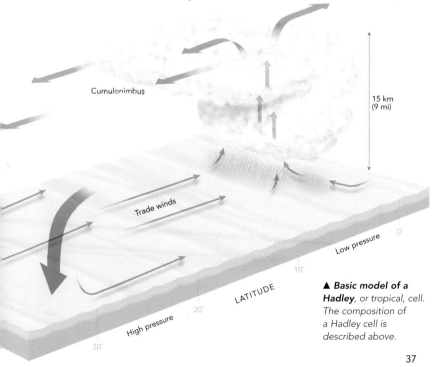

Cumulonimbus

15 km
(9 mi)

Trade winds

Low pressure

0°

10°

LATITUDE

High pressure

20°

30°

▲ *Basic model of a* **Hadley**, *or tropical, cell. The composition of a Hadley cell is described above.*

1. Low-level currents of air that flow polewards from the subtropical highs. This warm, moist air forms the warm sectors of middle-latitude frontal depressions that run across the middle- and high-latitude oceans, for example.
2. A region of rising air, at around 50–60°N and 50–60°S, represented by the large-scale rise of the warm, moist air in frontal depressions. This is the flow of tropical maritime air across gently sloping warm fronts. These common frontal depressions are the major source of precipitation for middle- and higher-latitude areas of the world, for example over much of western Europe, the southern Andes and South Island, New Zealand.
3. Like the ITCZ, this is a region of convergence at the surface, where air flows together from different directions, ascending to produce cloud and often widespread rain, drizzle and sometimes snow. Unlike the ITCZ, however, the winds carry less moisture. Those from higher latitudes are particularly cool and quite dry.
4. A return flow in the upper troposphere that heads towards the upper outflow from the ITCZ. These two flows converge above the subtropical highs, and are matched by the two currents that diverge directly below them at the surface.

Polar cell

The final component of vertical air circulation is the weak Polar cell. This comprises:

▼ *Basic model of a* **Ferrel**, *or middle-latitude cell. The composition of a Ferrel cell is explained above.*

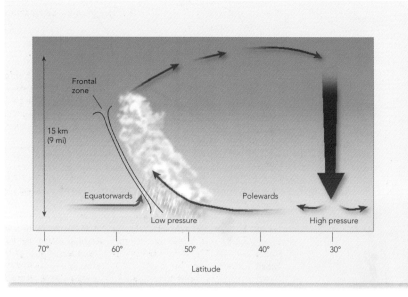

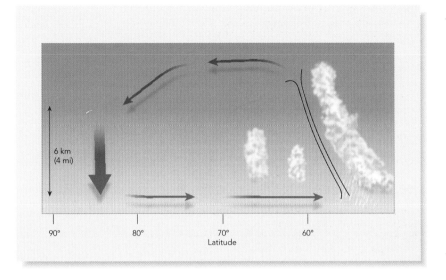

90°   80°   70°   60°
Latitude

6 km
(4 mi)

▲ *Basic model of a*
Polar cell. *The*
composition of a Polar
cell is detailed here.

1. Gentle sinking in the highest latitudes, associated with surface highs.
2. Surface flow towards the equator, some of which ultimately undercuts the warm-sector tropical maritime air in the frontal zone. This forms the leading edge of the polar air behind a cold front.
3. A weak return flow from above frontal depressions towards the poles.

SURFACE TEMPERATURES

There is a great seasonal variation in the amount of solar radiation received at the surface of the planet, especially at the higher latitudes. The tropics do not see as large a change. These differences are mirrored in the seasonal change of ocean surface temperature and the temperature over the continents.

January

Consider the difference in air temperature between a couple of equatorial locations and two high-latitude sites, using the mean air temperature for January.

The January average temperature over the Democratic Republic of the Congo, at 15°E on the equator, is around 25°C (77°F), while at the same longitude in northern Norway it is about –10°C (14°F). Now compare a site in Amazonian Brazil, at 60°W on the equator, with one in northwestern Greenland at the same longitude. The average temperatures

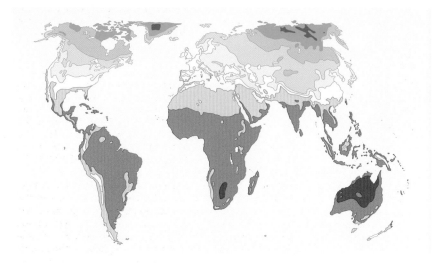

at these two places are about 25°C (77°F) and –30°C (–22°F) respectively.

Therefore, in January, we would expect to see a temperature difference between the equator and high latitudes in the winter hemisphere of about 35–55°C (65–100°F). The coldest temperatures in January are not centred on the pole, but typically occur in northeastern Russia. The Siberian city of Verkhoyansk experiences a January mean temperature of –40°C (–40°F), and on 6 February 1933 recorded the record lowest northern hemisphere minimum of –68°C (–90°F).

Mild west, cold east coasts

It is clear from the temperature patterns that, in middle and high latitudes, the broad continents of the northern hemisphere are intensely cold in the winter. There is an east–west difference, however, with their eastern flanks colder than the western. This is true of both Eurasia and North America. The coldest conditions on the east coasts are caused by the prevailing winds, which blow off the cold continents. In contrast, the west coasts experience milder conditions in part because of the tropical maritime air borne by the travelling frontal lows that approach from the ocean. These are complemented by warm ocean currents that stream towards the western coasts.

January Heat

During January, on average the warmest places lie in the interior of South Africa and more widely over much of northern Australia, where the mean temperature is higher than 30°C (86°F). Darwin tends to be the hottest Australian state capital, with a mean maximum in January of 31.7°C (89°F). The middle-latitude and maritime capital, Hobart in Tasmania, can only muster 21.5°C (71°F) as its average. The record summer maximum in any Australian state capital belongs to Adelaide where, on 12 January 1939, the high reached 47.6°C (118°F). It is the outbreak of extremely hot air from the interior that leads to these baking temperatures.

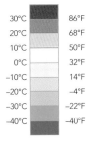

30°C	86°F
20°C	68°F
10°C	50°F
0°C	32°F
–10°C	14°F
–20°C	–4°F
–30°C	–22°F
–40°C	–40°F

◄ **January mean surface air** temperature over land. The broad continents of the northern hemisphere are extremely cold in the northern winter.

▼ **January mean air temperature** over land. The eastern coasts of the northern continents take the brunt of the cold in the winter.

Both the Gulf Stream/North Atlantic Drift and the Kuro Siwo/North Pacific Current are crucial in this respect (see January mean isobar/wind map on page 31 and January mean temperature map on page 40.

July

In July, the temperature contrasts between the equator and higher latitudes are quite different from those in January. The mean temperatures at the same points in the Congo and Amazonian Brazil are still around 25°C (77°F), while the matching values for northern Norway and Greenland are about 10°C (50°F) and 0°C (32°F) respectively. This means that the differences are between 15°C (27°F) and 25°C (45°F) – or something like half of those seen in winter.

This change in the temperature gradient from low to high latitudes holds for both hemispheres and throughout the depth of the troposphere. The approximate doubling of the difference from summer to winter is mainly due to the dramatic change from polar day to polar night. During the long polar night, vast areas of the highest latitudes cool substantially, while during the long days of the summer, temperatures reach significantly higher levels.

Conservative tropics

In general, the tropics experience a very small annual temperature range between the warmest and coolest months, because there is little variation in the amount of solar radiation received throughout the year. This is why the different seasons within the tropics are defined by when it rains, rather than by temperature changes. In contrast, throughout the extratropics, the winter is significantly colder than the summer, so the annual round of warming and cooling is a basic means of defining the seasons.

30°C	86°F
20°C	68°F
10°C	50°F
0°C	32°F
–10°C	14°F
–20°C	–4°F
–30°C	–22°F
–40°C	–40°F

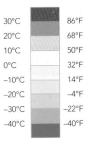

In July, the hottest conditions are found on the continents that have extensive tracts with mean air temperatures above 30°C (86°F). It is within the most extensive of these, across Saharan Africa, that the world's highest temperatures have been observed. As in the southern continents in January, these hot areas are partly related to their distance from the influence of air flowing from the oceans, and also to the presence of the sinking air of the Hadley cells (see page 36). The deep sinking motion in the subtropics is characterized by extensive clear skies promoting very high temperatures during the day, and chilly conditions at night in the 'hot' deserts of the world.

In hot coastal regions, however, such as the Persian Gulf, overnight temperatures remain high because of the generally very humid air. The water vapour in this air absorbs some of the upward Earth radiation and re-radiates part of it back to the surface, acting as a form of insulator. This is an example of the Greenhouse Effect, in which gases such as water vapour and carbon dioxide keep surface temperatures higher than they would otherwise be (see pages 131–137).

Highest Mean Annual Temperature
The world's highest screen maximum (temperatures measured in a weather screen, see pages 92–93), was 58°C (136°F) on 13 September 1922 at Al Aziziya, just south of Tripoli in Libya. The highest mean annual screen temperature is 34.4°C (94°F), from 1960 to 1966 at Dallol, in the low-lying Danakil Depression that straddles Ethiopia and Eritrea.

PRECIPITATION

The global pattern of annual precipitation is strongly related to those of pressure and wind.

In middle latitudes, widespread (spanning hundreds of kilometres) precipitation is generated by the ascent of warm, moist air over fronts (see page 56) that sweep across the oceans and adjacent continents. Frontal rain and snow move with the frontal depressions (see page 57) that create them. In many of the regions in the middle latitudes these travelling disturbances provide much of the rain and snow. The areas of activity vary seasonally: they tend to shift towards the pole in the summer months.

These systems are responsible for a good deal of the precipitation along the extreme western flank of North America, from the Gulf of Mexico to the Maritime Provinces of Canada, and also across much of Europe, including the Mediterranean in the autumn and winter. They also affect regions from China and Japan to Kamchatka in Russia, as well as over and to the west of the southern Andes, as well as southeastern South America in

Lowest Mean Annual Temperature
The world's lowest mean annual screen temperature of –57.8°C (–72°F) belongs to the Russian Antarctic station of Polus Nedostupnosti. A contributing factor to this amazingly low value is the extreme dryness that accompanies frigidly cold air. There is virtually no water vapour in the atmosphere above the Antarctic and, therefore, no 'greenhouse' contribution from that source.

the autumn and winter to the southern flanks of southern Africa. Australia and New Zealand are affected during their cooler season. These depressions produce widespread precipitation over the middle-latitude oceans as well.

During the summer, over middle-latitude continents, strong surface heating leads to significant showery rain. This tends to be shorter-lived and heavier than the frontal type.

Wet and snowy mountains

Annual totals indicate that some 500–2,000 mm (20–80 in) of precipitation falls across Europe in a typical year. The largest amounts occur in mountainous regions, especially those that abut the Atlantic Ocean and provide the first landfall for the travelling frontal systems. Broadly similar totals occur across western North America, with heavier falls concentrated along the relatively narrow mountainous coastal zone from central California northwards. The steep rain/snowfall gradient across this strip reflects the impact these massive coastal ranges have on frontal precipitation and the rain-shadow region to the east, where totals are below 250 mm (10 in) (see page 34).

These mountainous regions also face the onslaught of winter depressions and suffer the snowiest conditions. These large totals are partly an expression of orographic enhancement (see page 74) and the fact that much of the precipitation boosted in this way literally 'scavenges' water that could have fallen downstream. This phenomenon is

World Record Snowfall

The world record annual snow total comes from Paradise Ranger Station on Mount Rainier in Washington State, USA, where 31.102 m (102.4 ft) fell between 19 February 1991 and 18 February 1992.

▼ *Snow-capped Rocky Mountains* in Colorado, USA. Taken as part of the Rocky Mountain snow survey from NOAA aircraft. The large snow and rainfall totals on the Rockies, demonstrate the influence these massive coastal ranges have on frontal precipitation.

related to the rain shadow areas of the world – that are commonly downstream of mountains and hills with regard to predominant wind direction.

Dry areas

The pattern of dry areas (with less than 500 mm – 20 inches in a year, for example) can be related to a number of causes. At the highest of northern latitudes, low precipitation values are due, in part, to the low temperatures that prevail in those regions, because the amount of water vapour contained in cold air is very small. Even if the atmosphere provides a means of lifting the air to cool it enough for the water vapour to condense into clouds, little rain or snow is produced (see page 65).

The aridity of the middle-latitude continental interiors is partly due to a rain-shadow effect: for example, the high plains of the United States, and the dry region of western Argentina, in the lee of the Andes. Other areas, such as Siberia in Russia, which is east of the Urals and north of the Himalayas, are generally arid because, in winter, the massive anticyclone (see January map of Asia, page 26) suppresses any ascent and is very cold. In summer, surface heating will spark off scattered showery precipitation, but the region's remoteness from the sea means that very humid air rarely reaches it.

In contrast, the interior of the United States is exposed to very large incursions of moist air from the Gulf of Mexico. During the summer, these provide the essential ingredient of the torrential, thundery downpours that can be linked to severe phenomena like large hailstones (see page 158) or even tornadoes (see page 161).

▼ *The impact of water vapour on night time cooling under clear skies. The extreme dryness over the desert promotes substantial long-wave cooling and quite chilly conditions. The more humid air flanking the Gulf means that some of the outgoing radiation is absorbed and re-radiated back down, to keep surface temperatures elevated.*

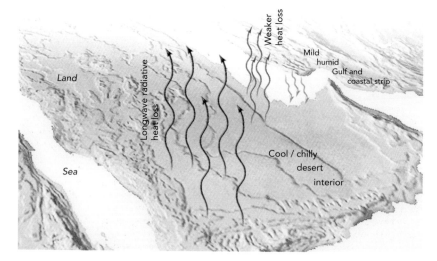

The marked aridity of the Sahara, Arabia and the Thar Desert of northwest India is essentially an expression of the sinking portion of the Hadley cell (see page 36). The same is true of the Australian and Kalahari Deserts, and indeed the regions of scant rainfall that stretch across the eastern tropical/ subtropical oceans.

Another group of arid land areas runs down western South America and Southern Africa. These are affected by the presence of cold ocean currents that flow towards the equator along the coasts. The Atacama and Namib Deserts are here, because the cold water suppresses any rain-producing ascent but lies under extensive layer cloud just offshore. In fact, at Calama in northern Chile, no rainfall at all was reported in a 400-year period up to 1971.

ITCZ

The most extensive regions of precipitation are within the tropics (see maps on pages 46–47). These areas are where the ITCZ (see pages 30–32) and its deep convective clouds hold sway. Sometimes, hurricanes and typhoons are created within the regime of the Trade Winds, producing widespread heavy rain as well as their notoriously dangerous winds.

Those places where 2,000–3,000 mm (80–120 in) and more are observed are regions:
1. where the ITCZ is active;
2. where mountainous coasts face onshore flow – particularly in monsoon areas (see page 156) such as western India and Sierra Leone;
3. where hurricanes, typhoons or cyclones (Indian Ocean) run across land areas;
4. and where mountainous islands like Indonesia trigger locally heavy showers.

Much of the heavy rainfall that falls across Southeast Asia and West Africa is monsoonal, while some of the large amounts over the Caribbean, Central America, the Phillipines, Vietnam northwards to Japan, and Madagascar are produced by intense tropical cyclones. These travelling rotating storms tend to be embedded in the larger-scale northeast and southeast Trades. Often, they are born on the eastern flanks of oceans and make landfall on their western flanks.

This annual pattern masks the seasonal migration of the ITCZ, so the heavy rainfall over Southeast Asia occurs during the summer monsoon. Conditions during the winter monsoon are mainly dry.

Rainfall in the Tropics

With the very high humidity levels within the oceanic tropics, and the intense surface heating there, it is no surprise that the world's rainfall records are held by the region. The largest rainfall total for any 12-month period was recorded in Cherrapunji in the Indian tea-growing region of Assam. It returned an accumulation of 26.27 m (86.2 ft) from August 1860 to July 1861. The same station also holds the wettest month record: 2.93 m (9.6 ft) in July 1861. The largest 24-hour fall comes from the island of Réunion in the western Indian Ocean, where an unbelievable 1.87 m (6.1 ft) was recorded during 15–16 March 1952.

45

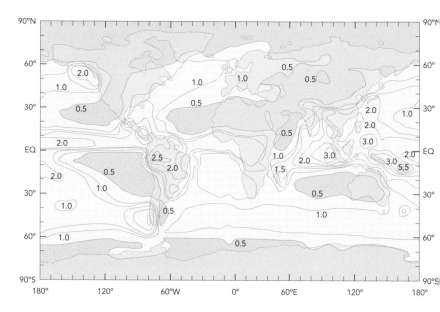

EL NIÑO

El Niño is nothing new – it has most probably occurred intermittently for thousands of years. When El Niño rages, it has a very significant widespread impact over a few seasons. Scientists are gradually unravelling its secrets, using improved monitoring and advanced modelling techniques. Atmospheric scientists are today aware of the nature of the phenomenon. They understand how an event in the equatorial Pacific somehow pervades the atmosphere to force significant seasonal anomalies of temperature and rain some thousands of kilometres distant. How this occurs, and which regions are affected, are discussed in pages 8–23.

The term 'El Niño' is Spanish for 'the little boy', and its use to label a significant but local ocean-warming event in the coastal region of Peru and Ecuador dates from a few centuries ago. However, the earliest written evidence of what was probably El Niño-related weather in South America comes from the Spanish colonists who settled in these regions during the late 15th century.

The name was coined by fishermen whose livelihood was affected by the annual appearance of a warm ocean current, typically around Christmas time (hence 'El Niño', the term also used for the Christ Child), which persisted in the region for a few months. One outcome was that fish – anchovies, for example – were scarcer during this period; anchovies and other fish ordinarily fed in the nutrient-rich cool water that

▲ *Regions where mean annual precipitation is less than 0.5 m (1.6 ft) are coloured in purple. Measurements are shown in metres.*

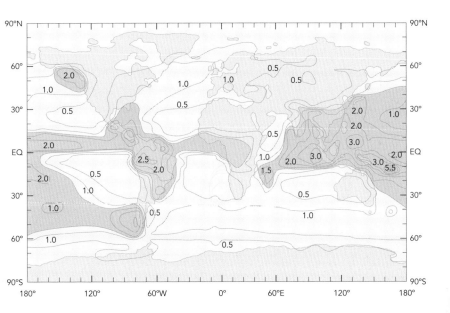

90°N   90°N

▲ **Regions where mean annual** precipitation exceeds 1.5 m (5 ft) are coloured brown. Measurements are shown in metres.

was ordinarily present offshore but they did not linger in the absence of available food. Such fish were a staple of the local economy, which suffered as a result.

Over the years, the term 'El Niño' has been applied to the larger-scale and more intense ocean warming that occurs occasionally across huge stretches of the equatorial Pacific. Today, the marked warming near Peru and Ecuador, which was noted all those years ago, is known to be only a relatively local signature of a Pacific-wide change. In fact, on occasion, El Niño leads to very substantial thermal and rainfall anomalies in areas far from the Pacific Ocean.

The Southern Oscillation

El Niño is associated with an atmospheric phenomenon known as the Southern Oscillation (SO). This term was coined by Sir Gilbert Walker in 1923, when he was assigned to the Indian Meteorological Department. In an effort to find a way of predicting the character of the Asian summer monsoon, he studied large-scale pressure variations and discovered that when pressure is high in part of the Pacific Ocean, it tends to be low in the Indian Ocean from Africa to Australia.

Pressure is normally high over the southeast Pacific and low in the western equatorial Pacific. The horizontal gradient of pressure between these two centres leads to the presence of the easterly (westward-blowing) Trade Winds. During such times, the SO is said to be in its High Index.

47

Sometimes, however, the barometer falls over a period of months across the southeastern Pacific and, when this happens, it rises simultaneously in the western Pacific. This change leads to a weakening of the pressure gradient, together with a weakening – or even a reversal – of the Trades. This is known as the Low Index of the SO. Walker noted that during such phases, there were droughts in Australia, Indonesia, India and parts of Africa. In addition, winters tended to be unusually warm in western Canada. Furthermore, the desert islands in the middle equatorial Pacific suffered persistent and torrential rains.

ENSO

In the late 1960s, Professor Jacob Bjerknes was the first to suggest a possible link between the SO phenomenon and El Niño. He proposed that the unusually warm sea-surface temperatures across stretches of the equatorial Pacific were probably related to the weak, or even reversed, easterlies and the torrential rain of the Low Index phase. Bjerknes showed that the SO and El Niño are both parts of the same phenomenon, known collectively as ENSO. Today, an SO index is quoted – the difference in monthly mean-sea-level pressure between Tahiti, representing the South Pacific anti-cyclone, and Darwin, representing the western Pacific low.

Normal conditions

During normal, or average years, the easterly winds that blow along the equator, and the southeasterlies that blow along the coast of Ecuador and Peru, drag surface water along with them. The rotation of the Earth deflects this water to the right of the flow in the northern hemisphere, and to the left in the southern. This means that water is driven away from the equator in both hemispheres and also from the Peru/Ecuador coastline. Cold, nutrient-rich water wells up from below to replace it, forming narrow zones of equatorial and coastal upwelling less than 150 km (90 mi) wide.

▼ *The Southern Oscillation (SO).* This diagram depicts the slmultaneous rise in pressure at Darwin, Australia and fall in pressure at Tahiti.

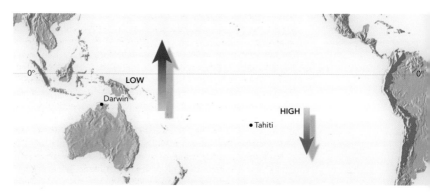

► **Surface pressure anomalies** *for Darwin, Australia and Tahiti, 1970–90. The red and blue lines represent the 20-year pattern of simultaneous rise and fall of pressure in each location.*

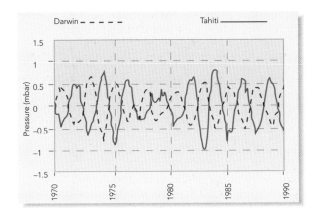

Normal conditions are marked by cool temperatures over the eastern Pacific and a warm maximum over the equatorial western Pacific. This western area is so warm that very deep convective cloud and heavy rainfall are a hallmark. Part of the huge volume of air that ascends to great height within these clouds – as high as the upper troposphere – moves eastwards at these levels and sinks in depth across the eastern Pacific. This vertical circulation is called a Walker cell, after Sir Gilbert Walker. A number of these cells exist around the equator, connecting wet and dry regions. The descending portions of such cells are characterized by very dry and often cloud-free weather.

Thermocline

Within the ocean there is a layer with a depth of 100 m (330 ft) or so, through which the water temperature drops rapidly. Known as the thermocline, it separates the upper warmer zone from the much colder deeper reaches.

Normally, the thermocline is near the surface in the eastern equatorial Pacific, some 50 m (160 ft) down, and it slopes gently down towards the western side, where it is found at a depth of about 200 m (660 ft). If there were no wind stress on the surface of the ocean, the thermocline would be nearly horizontal. In this region, however, the persistent Trades drive water westwards, lifting the thermocline towards the surface in the east, and depressing it in the west. The fact that the westward-driven surface water is steadily warmed by sunshine and, therefore, is of lower density, means that the surface of the sea slopes up towards the western equatorial Pacific. When the Trades are blowing at their strongest, the sea level in the western basin is over 0.5 m (1.6 ft) higher than in the east. This very broad, flattened mound of warm water occurs around Indonesia and New Guinea.

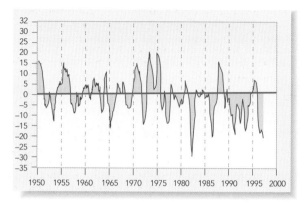

◀ **Smoothed values** of the Southern Oscillation (SO) Index. Negative values indicate warm ENSO phases. Note the marked 1982/1983 and 1997/1998 events.

As the SO index gradually moves to a low-value phase, when the Tahiti/Darwin difference is small, the relaxation in the normally strong Trades leads to the thermocline becoming less tilted. It drops by more than 100 m (330 ft) in the east and cuts off the cool, upwelled water from the Ecuador/Peru coastal zone. Thus, the sea level flattens out along the equator, falling in the west and rising in the east. In association with this, the warm surface water flows eastwards as a long, low wave known as a Kelvin wave, reaching South America a few months later, where it turns north and south along the coast. This leads to an increase in sea level and the migration of fish. The northward branch of warm water influences marine life as far north as Vancouver, Canada.

The eastward migration of the warm water across the equatorial Pacific causes the air above it to become moist and warm. It also gains sufficient buoyancy to produce massive convective cloud and torrential rain in regions that otherwise are persistently arid.

El Niño effects

The classic El Niño conditions include unusually high rainfall across the central equatorial ocean, as well as unusually dry conditions over the western sector, including northern South America, eastern Australia and over Indonesia. This distinct pattern is due to the fact

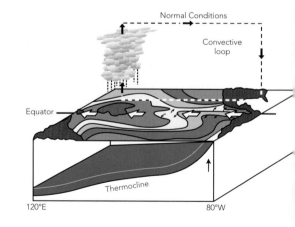

that one portion of the enormous upward movement of air in the displaced convective region subsides over the western Pacific.

After the Kelvin wave has left the western Pacific, the warm water layer thins substantially and mixes with cooler water. This cooling leads to less evaporation and a more stable atmosphere, which together mean less rain. The eastern half of Australia and all of Indonesia, therefore, are susceptible to drought during a marked El Niño.

There are other typical thermal and precipitation anomalies associated with a strong El Niño. The period from June to August that follows the evolution of the El Niño tends to be characterized by drier than average conditions around Indonesia, Australia and the Fijian Islands. Drought is a risk across the northern part of South America and the southern Caribbean, too – and there is evidence that the Indian monsoon may be drier. The extensive forest fires that affected large areas of Indonesia and Malaysia in September 1997 were related, in part, to the unusually dry preceding months, influenced by El Niño, and stable weather conditions around that time. Wet conditions occur in the central equatorial Pacific because of the significantly higher sea-surface temperature.

The period from December to February also illustrates the major tropical pattern that is linked to shifts in location and intensity of the Walker cells. Dry conditions stretch from Sumatra and southern Malaysia to the Hawaiian Islands in the north, and the Fijian Islands in the south. Additionally, drought is a high risk for eastern equatorial South America and southeastern Africa.

Abnormally wet conditions occur over Ecuador, Peru, southern Brazil, Uruguay, northern Argentina, southern USA and equatorial east Africa. Warmer than average winter

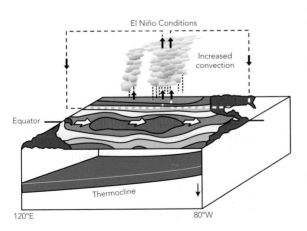

◀ **Normal (left) and El Niño (right)** *conditions, including sea surface temperature (blue is cold, brown is warm), thermocline depth and Walker cell location (depicted by the arrows). During El Niño, the warm surface water flows east along the equator, bringing thunderstorms.*

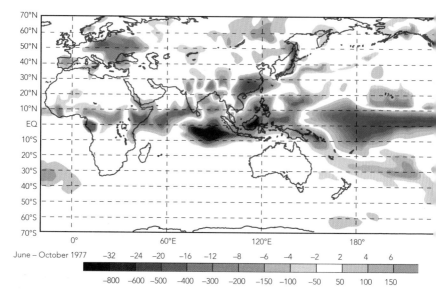

June – October 1977

| −32 | −24 | −20 | −16 | −12 | −8 | −6 | −4 | −2 | 2 | 4 | 6 |

| −800 | −600 | −500 | −400 | −300 | −200 | −150 | −100 | −50 | 50 | 100 | 150 |

conditions are often experienced from Alaska to the Canadian Rockies, in parts of southeastern Canada and northeastern USA, and around Japan.

El Niño's global impact

It is clear how El Niño is able to influence the weather patterns within the tropics, but how does it produce wet weather in San Francisco, Tampa or Buenos Aires? The answer lies in the impact that the unusually located, deep tropical rain clouds have on the upper atmosphere.

The deep clouds that move across to the central equatorial Pacific pump very large amounts of heat and air high up into the troposphere, over a very extensive region. Shifting the thunderstorms from the western Pacific to a point thousands of kilometres farther east strengthens the upper tropospheric flow significantly.

The change in the strength and pattern of the winds at 200 mbar can be highlighted by comparing the average picture for January with that of January 1998 (see page 55). The strength of the jet – that relatively narrow 'ribbon' of fast-flowing air in the upper troposphere – increased notably across both the North Pacific and southeastern USA. There are also more subtle, but nevertheless significant, changes in the wind direction depicted by the thin streamlines with arrowheads. The more vigorous, wavy jet means that there is a likelihood of more active frontal systems (wetter and windier) that may be marginally, but significantly, displaced from their normal location.

▲ **Estimated rainfall anomalies** for June to October 1997. Wetter weather is indicated in green, drier weather is indicated in brown. The 1997 to 1998 El Niño season produced particularly unstable weather conditions.

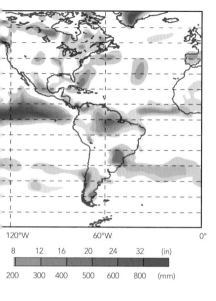

120°W   60°W   0°

| 8 | 12 | 16 | 20 | 24 | 32 | (in) |

| 200 | 300 | 400 | 500 | 600 | 800 | (mm) |

The cost

Marked El Niños do not occur regularly. Recently, the world has seen two dramatically influential examples of the El Niño phenomenon – in 1982–83 and 1997–98. Because they are associated with extreme regional weather events that persist for a season or so, they are costly. The 1982–83 El Niño was estimated to have caused extensive damage, costing some US$8,110 million globally (see table on page 54)

Because an El Niño grows slowly over months and seasons, and can be monitored from weather satellites and a special surface network of observation sites across the equatorial Pacific, timely warnings of the risk of abnormal conditions can be issued well ahead of the event. The characteristic anomalies that we are aware of form one basis for such warnings. In addition, climate modelling

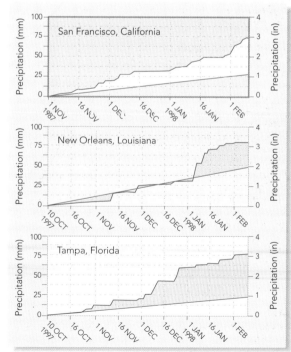

▶ **Observed (October 1997** to early February 1998) and average accumulated rainfall for three US cities. All three cities experienced increased rainfall during the El Niño.

and prediction centres use sophisticated computer models to issue predictions of the likely outbreak, evolution and decline of an El Niño. This means that, potentially at least, governments in countries that are likely to see anomalously low rainfall in association with an El Niño can plan for such an event. For example, in the Australian summer during such times, there is an enhanced risk of below-average rainfall across the eastern part of the nation. This implies a heightened risk of bushfires that can encroach on cities such as Sydney. The state and city authorities will be aware of the necessity for greater preparedness than is required for an 'average' year.

La Niña

The equatorial Pacific not only experiences El Niño however; on occasion it can experience its antithesis known as 'La Niña', or 'the baby girl'.

During La Niña the central and eastern tropical Pacific waters tend to become much cooler than average. La Niña is also linked to generally cooler than average surface land temperatures across the tropics and subtropics. There is also evidence of increased tropical storm activity in the North Atlantic during La Niña and decreased activity during El Niño. The 1997–8 El Niño decayed rapidly during January to April 1998, and in May and June the sea surface thermal anomaly in the central equatorial Pacific changed from one degree Celsius above to one below the long-term average. La Niña's cold-ocean pattern then developed during the second half of 1998.

As this evolved, large-scale rainfall patterns were changing as expected to under such conditions. Relatively wet weather occurred across large areas of Indonesia, Australia and southern Africa, while lower than average rainfall was observed over southern Brazil, Uruguay, northern Argentina and east Africa. La Niña is also linked to generally cooler than average surface land temperatures across the tropics and subtropics.

There is also evidence of increased tropical storm activity in the North Atlantic during La Niña and decreased activity during El Niño.

▶ Mean location and speed of 250 mbar winds (streamline and isotachs) for December to February 1979–1995 (first map), compared to the December 1997 to February 1998 El Niño year (second diagram). The difference between the two is shown in the last map where the more vigorous jetstream during an El Niño can lead to frontal systems that are marginally, but significantly displaced.

THE COST OF THE 1982–83 EL NIÑO

Flooding

US Gulf States	$1,270 million
Ecuador/Northern Peru	$650 million
Bolivia	$300 million
Cuba	$170 million

Hurricanes

Hawaii	$230 million
Tahiti	$50 million

Drought/fires

Australia	$2,500 million
Southern Africa	$1,000 million
Mexico/Central America	$600 million
Indonesia	$500 million
Philippines	$450 million
Southern Peru/Western Bolivia	$240 million
Southern India/Sri Lanka	$150 million

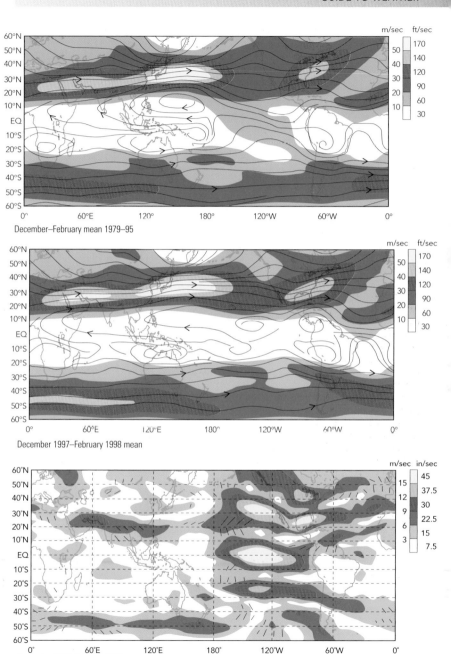

December–February mean 1979–95

December 1997–February 1998 mean

December 1997–February 1998 anomaly

What makes the wind blow? How do clouds form and stay in the sky? How do they produce rain, snow and drizzle? Why are there different types of fog? How do dew and frost form? These are some of the topics discussed in this chapter.

FRONTAL SYSTEMS

Fronts are significant weather features in middle and higher latitudes. Fronts are shallow sloping zones that separate extensive air masses that have different values of temperature and humidity. Cold and warm fronts are the leading edges of cold and warm air masses that sweep generally towards lower or higher latitudes respectively.

▶ *Idealized cloud sequence* associated with a warm front. The cloud formation changes as the warm front approaches, moving through from high cirrus to low nimbostratus.

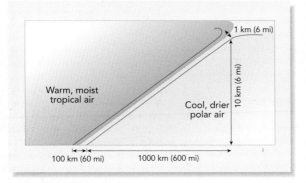

1 km (6 mi)

Warm, moist
tropical air

Cool, drier
polar air

10 km (6 mi)

100 km (60 mi)   1000 km (600 mi)

◀ *Idealized vertical cross-section* of a front. Broadly, the arrival of a warm front brings, warmer, but moister air. Any weather change is likely to be gradual.

Typically, a front slopes at about 1 in 100, with cold fronts somewhat steeper and warm fronts somewhat shallower. A front is normally about 1 km deep (about half a mile), which means that it intersects the surface across a region some 100 km (60 mi) wide. Therefore, the weather changes associated with a front do not normally occur instantly, but gradually over a transition zone.

Broadly, the passage of a warm front brings warmer, moister air and a veering of the wind direction. This means that the wind shifts in a clockwise direction, typically over the space of an hour or so, from southeasterly to southwesterly in the northern hemisphere; in the southern hemisphere, the wind will shift from northeasterly to southwesterly.

▶ *Typical rain region* ahead of a surface warm front. Interspersed light and heavy rain occurs within a region of 300 km (200 mi) ahead of the front.

Warm fronts

The area ahead of an approaching warm front is often influenced by the signs of the advancing warm, moist air as it glides across the sloping zone between the two air masses. In fact, much of the warm air streams beyond the line where the front meets the surface. High above the Earth's surface, the first signs of cirrus cloud will occur. This can be as far as 600–700 km (370–430 mi) ahead of the warm front at the surface.

▶ *Typical rain region* ahead of a surface cold front. Heavy rain occurs up to 50 km (30 mi) ahead of the front.

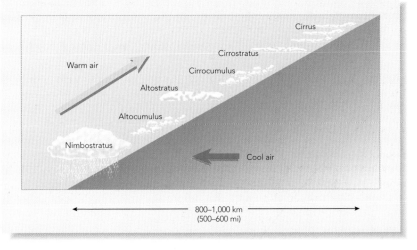

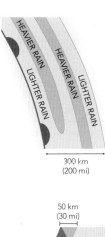

As the warm front approaches a point on the surface, the base of the cloud produced by the overrunning warm, moist tropical air gradually lowers. This is indicated by the gradual progression from cirrus to cirrostratus/cirrocumulus, followed by altostratus/altocumulus and a thickening into nimbostratus, which will produce precipitation that reaches the surface.

Closer to the surface, the rain falling through the very damp layer below the nimbostratus cloud will evaporate a little, cooling the air slightly as a result. Sometimes, this process leads to condensation in the damp air, creating 'scud', or fractostratus, clouds. These are the ragged low clouds that fly across the sky during conditions of strong winds and moderate or heavy rain.

The leading edge of the warm frontal rain can occur some 200–300 km (120–180 mi) ahead of the surface front and cause a few hours of precipitation before the arrival of the warm sector air. Precipitation rates in this region would be something like a few millimetres an hour, although radar observations reveal that rain bands often occur, with heavier, localized bursts.

This describes the progression of a typical warm front. In reality, however, each front is different. The cloud sequence may not follow the same pattern, and the warm frontal rain band may be, for example, less extensive, or slower moving.

The warm sector

The region between a warm and cold front is known as the warm sector. Quite often, it is characterized by extensive layer cloud that can produce persistently miserable conditions on exposed coasts, but may break up into pleasantly sunny conditions to the lee of hills.

The relative warmth, dampness and cloudiness of a warm sector are an expression of the air's origin in oceanic regions of much lower latitudes. Precipitation within this sector is generally widespread; many frontal depressions exhibit a band of enhanced activity ahead of, and parallel to, the surface cold front. Visibility is often poor to moderate, and hill fog can be a problem in upland areas where the extensive low cloud has a base that is below the tops of hilly areas.

Behind the cold front

The passage of a cold front, as its name implies, usually produces a drop in temperature and dewpoint. This leads to cooler and drier conditions, in terms of absolute humidity or the amount of water vapour in the air.

The polar air that streams across the surface behind a cold front generally provides better visibility because it is often unstable, turning over in great depth and becoming well mixed. This instability also produces showery weather, with short-lived precipitation falling from deep cumulus clouds. These characteristics are common over middle- and high-latitude oceans, but not over continental areas like North America. There, cold air that sweeps southwards from Canada in the winter does not experience significant surface heating over the cold land surface, and tends not to generate deep convective cloud.

In general, as a cold front passes, the wind veers from southwesterly to westerly or northwesterly in the northern hemisphere; in the southern hemisphere, it tends to shift from northwesterly to southwesterly.

▶ **NOAA weather satellite** *thermal image of a partly occluded frontal depression in the northeast Atlantic. Occluded fronts occur when a cold front catches up with the warm front and 'scoops' the warm moist air up away from the surface.*

▼ **Broken stratus cloud** *in a warm sector. Layered cloud such as stratus is often produced in the region between a warm and cold front.*

Occluded fronts

During the lifecycle of frontal systems, occlusions naturally evolve. An occluded front is a front with warm air lifted off the surface, with cool or cold air at lower levels. Because a cold front travels faster, it tends to scoop the warm air up away from the surface when it catches up with the warm front. This 'occlusion' grows in length with time until a low, in its dying stages, is fully occluded. At the same time, deep layers of warm, moist air ascend continuously over the gently inclined warm and cold fronts, to produce very extensive condensation in the form of cloud.

Conveyor belts

Frontal systems have characteristic large-scale currents of air that move in an organized fashion. The major cloud-producing flow is called the warm conveyor belt, which streams through the warm sector ahead of the cold front. It ascends gradually from a kilometre or so above the ground surface,

▼ *Typical wind* **change** *across a cold front in the Northern and Southern Hemispheres.*

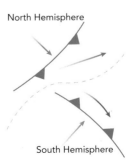

North Hemisphere

South Hemisphere

59

in the southwestern part of the sector (northwestern part in southern hemisphere frontal lows), as its runs parallel to the front, eventually flowing over the warm front up to 5 or 6 km (3 or 4 mi) above the surface.

This feature is called a conveyor belt because it transports most of the all-important heat and moisture associated with frontal depressions. The very large thermal difference between the tropics and extratropics drives the atmosphere and ocean to act in such a way that they propel warmer fluid polewards and cooler fluid equatorwards. This is, therefore, an expression of the 'requirement' that the air and the sea act in a real sense as convectors, transporting heat towards high latitudes within their bodily motion (see pages 22–23).

The warm conveyor belt is closely related to the massive region of cloud within the warm sector and above the warm front. This cloud is the 'signature' of huge volumes of tropical maritime air that flow polewards and upwards within the frontal system. Both movements act to cool the air.

There is also a cold conveyor belt, which consists of air that actually approaches the warm front from ahead and sinks to move parallel to the front, undercutting the higher

▲ *Large-scale frontal system* flow relative to a partly occluded depression in the middle latitudes.

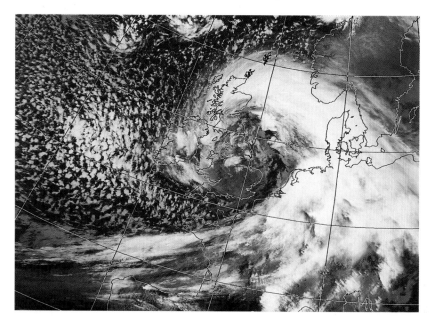

warm conveyor belt. Then, it ascends into the occluded front. A third current flows through the middle troposphere, overrunning the travelling low as a cold, dry stream of air.

Behind the cold front, a huge volume of cool, relatively dry polar air streams across the surface. Over the ocean areas that are commonly downstream of air blowing off cold wintertime continents, a great deal of heat and moisture is pumped up into the atmosphere when it flows across the generally warmer sea. Here, the depression is transporting cold, dry air equatorwards, and air that flows towards the equator tends to sink, becoming compressed. As a result, it is warmed by two processes: convection, and compression warming of the air that sinks between the convective clouds.

This action is visible as a region of widespread, scattered convective cumulus clouds that rise essentially as bubbles from over the sea. They often produce showers, separated by bright spells, caused by the sinking air.

PRESSURE AND WIND

The difference between high and low pressure across the Earth's surface is the basic driving force that makes the air move.

Take as an example the difference in pressure between the centres of the Iceland Low and Azores High during the North Atlantic winter, assessed using the extreme-season maps. This turns out to be about 25 mbar. By determining the distance between the two, which is something like 2,500 km (1,500 mi), we have the information necessary to calculate the horizontal gradient of pressure – or how fast pressure changes across the sea surface. In this case, it would be around 1 mbar per 100 km (60 mi). This is a fairly steep gradient and means that the sea-surface wind speed midway

◄ Thermal infrared satellite image of the frontal cloud and scattered showers of the Burns' Day storm over the UK. (See pages 164–166)

► Examples of the connection between pressure gradients and wind strength.
A: Steep pressure gradient (strong wind).
B: Gentle pressure gradient (weak wind)

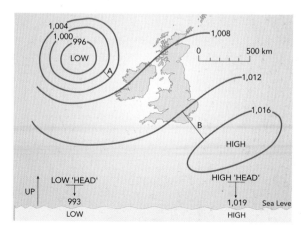

between the Azores and Iceland is, on average during the winter, about 16 m/sec or some 35 or 36 mi/hr (56–58 km/hr).

A large pressure difference between a high and a low that are close will produce a steep gradient and a strong force to drive the air. A much weaker gradient, however, will generate less force. The steeper the gradient, the stronger the wind.

The difference between the 'head' of air above a high and that above a low drives the air from the high towards the low. This flow will decrease the mass of air in the column above the high, causing pressure to fall, and will increase the mass of air in the region of the low, causing pressure to rise.

Although air flows from high-pressure regions towards low-pressure areas, the direction of the flow, or wind, is not straight from one to the other. The Earth's rotation causes the wind to be deflected so that it spirals out of the highs and into the lows. The direction of the mean prevailing winds across the Earth's surface in January and July is strongly related to the direction of the isobars. Isobars are graphic representations of this wind on weather maps (see page 116): smooth lines that connect places that have the same value of mean sea-level barometric pressure. They usually are drawn with 'standard' values such as 1,000 mbar plus or minus 4 mbar (e.g. 996 and 1,004 mbar). However, the winds do not flow exactly parallel to the isobars, but cut across them at an angle, in keeping with their spiralling nature.

At the surface and through the lower troposphere, air spiralling out of an anticyclone (see page 25) must be replaced by air that is slowly sinking within the high. It follows that air spiralling into regions of low pressure must ascend. These rising and sinking motions are very important, for without them, there would be no weather as we know it.

Anticyclones are characterized by deeply sinking air, while cyclones exhibit large-scale ascending streams, often reaching great height. The extensive rising motion in cyclones tends to produce cloud, and rain or snow, the ascent of moist air being nature's favourite way of producing these weather features. In high-pressure regions, however, the large-scale descent of air generally gives dry conditions, although extensive low-layer cloud may also occur.

▲ *The link between descent/surface* outflow and ascent/surface inflow. The Earth's rotation causes air to spiral out of the high pressure areas into low pressure areas. Air that circulates out of the high pressure region ascends on a large scale.

Regional winds

There are many such winds too numerous to mention. All are related to the critical location of low and high pressure systems that act to channel the airflow in a particular direction. Local topography can also accentuate its strength by 'squeezing' wind between two areas of high ground.

In some parts of the world, such as areas of the Mediterranean basin, well-known winds blow over quite restricted areas. They occur when the pressure patterns display a particular distribution – like the northerly Mistral that shoots down the Rhone valley in southern France between a slow or stationary low pressure system over, say, central Europe and a high located across Biscay.

There are many regional winds around the Mediterranean, including the hot, dry southerly Sirocco whose baking heat comes from its source over the Sahara. In contrast, the wintertime northeasterly Bora is associated with the cold, gusty conditions found across the Adriatic shores of the Dinaric Alps.

There is also the Santa Ana wind of southern California. This hot, dry, northeasterly blows parchingly over the Los Angeles basin and is frequently linked to the wildfires that are a notorious risk for properties on the upwind flanks of that city.

▼ *Santa Ana winds.*
This view from the NASA Multi-angle Imaging SpectroRadiometer shows the pattern of airborne dust stirred up by Santa Ana winds off the coast of California, USA, on February 9, 2002.

Staying Aloft

Water is heavy: near sea level, a cubic metre of air weighs about 1.2 kg (2.6 lb), while one of water weighs 1,000 kg (2,200 lb). Clouds stay aloft, despite the weight of the water, because they are associated with rising air.

Cloud Shape

A cloud's 'look' and extent are expressions of how the air has risen to produce them. Extensive layer cloud – like stratus or stratocumulus – are formed by widespread ascent that is relatively gentle. In contrast, puffy cumulus or cumulonimbus are related to strongly ascending air across a more limited area.

Sea breezes

Along many of the world's spring and summertime coastlines, cool, 'fresh' air often blows onshore as the sea breeze. Whether or not this occurs depends on the larger-scale weather pattern providing relatively light winds and mainly clear skies over a coastal region. If this is the case, the land surface will heat up quicker than the adjacent sea after sunrise, because water has a more sluggish thermal response to the sun shining on it. Throughout the early morning hours, the preferential heating of the land leads to a fall in the barometric pressure there. The pressure over the sea does not fall, however, but it remains relatively high and drives the sea air across the coast towards the low inland.

The greatest contrast between the air temperature above the land and sea occurs during the afternoon, with the warmest conditions over land. This means that the strength of the breeze is usually greatest during the afternoon and will decline gradually as the sun goes down. The all-important thermal difference across the coast means that in the tropics sea breezes can generate all year round, while in higher latitudes they are generally only warm-season phenomena.

Sea breezes have distinct leading edges that move inland more or less parallel to the coastline, quickest across low-lying areas. The 'front' has a lobe-like structure whose passage leads frequently to an abrupt fall of temperature (as the sea air is cooler) and increase in humidity (because the sea air is damper). The wind direction can change rapidly, too. Often the denser sea air, which may be up to 300 m (980 ft) to 400 m (1,300 ft) deep, scoops up the warmer land air ahead of it to produce a line of cumulus clouds that are organised parallel to the coast. Such clouds can produce showers along this sea breeze 'front'.

After dark, as the land surface cools more rapidly than the sea, the pressure difference switches to drive a gentle land breeze towards the sea through the night. It tends to be lighter than the daytime sea breeze because the temperature contrast is weaker at night.

Lake breezes

Under the same large-scale weather conditions as those that permit the genesis of sea and land breezes, broadly similar circulations can occur across the shores of sizeable lakes. The US Great Lakes, for example, experience daytime lake breezes during some spring and summer days, as air blows onto the surrounding land across their shores. This can also occur over many large lakes or inland seas, such as the Caspian and Black Seas.

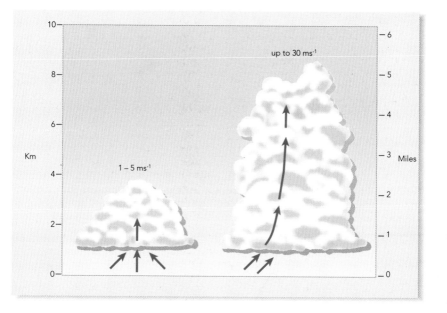

▲ Updraughts in cumulus clouds.
In general air ascends in small cumulus clouds at a rate of 1–5ms⁻¹, whereas large cumulonimbus clouds have air rushing through at up to 30 ms⁻¹.

CLOUDS

All clouds are formed by the cooling of moist air down to its dewpoint temperature, the temperature at which air must cool in order for saturation to occur. Further cooling causes the water vapour to condense gradually out of the air as myriad cloud droplets.

The amount of water vapour contained in saturated air depends on the air temperature. Cold air is capable of holding small amounts, while very warm air can contain much more. This marked increase in the saturation value of water vapour with temperature means that moist, cold air generally produces less precipitation than moist, warm air.

The most common way that damp air cools enough to produce cloud droplets or ice crystals is by ascending. In some cases, a volume of ascending air may be a few hundred

CLOUD PARTICLES			
	diameter (microns)	number (/m3)	fall speed (m/sec)
Cloud condensation nucleus	0.2	100,000,000	0.00001
Cloud droplet (typical)	20.0	1,000,000	0.01
Cloud droplet (large)	100.0	1000	0.27
Small drizzledrop	200.0	1000	0.70
Raindrop (typical)	2000.0	1	6.50

65

metres across (c.600 ft); in others, it may be as much as a thousand kilometres (c.600 mi) across. The speed with which air rises varies. In general, small cumulus clouds contain updraughts of between 1 and 5 m/sec (2 and 6 mi/hr), whereas cumulonimbus clouds may have air rushing up at 30 m/sec (65 mi/hr) or more in severe cases. In contrast, extensive layer cloud, formed by widespread ascent, is associated with air rising at between 5 and 20 cm/sec (up to half a mile an hour).

All cloud droplets have a nucleus around which they have condensed – known as the cloud condensation nucleus (CCN). These microscopic particles have a variety of sources, including blowing soil, volcanic eruptions, industry (e.g. smoke) and the spray from breaking waves. Their number varies from ocean to continent, and with height within the troposphere, but a typical value at sea level is around 100–200 million in every cubic metre (or every 35 cubic feet).

Cloud droplets vary in size depending, for example, on the number of such condensation nucleii, how much water vapour there is available, and the strength of the up-currents within the cloud. The incredibly tiny cloud droplets are so small that their terminal fallspeeds are much lower than the speed of the updraughts that create the clouds. They settle at about 1 cm/sec, while the larger ones do so at about 30 cm/sec (1 ft/sec). Generally, larger cloud droplets are found in convective clouds (cumulus clouds, formed by relatively warm air that pulls away from the Earth's surface; these generally fairly small clouds transport heat up into the atmosphere by the process of convection), where they can grow within the fast updraughts.

Cloud varieties

Meteorologists recognise a large variety of cloud types. They are defined in basic ways related to their essential shape: for example, a sheet or layer is 'stratiform', while those with lumpy upper surfaces and flat bases are 'cumuliform'.

HIGH

▲ *Cirrus* Tropics 6,000 to 18,000 m (20,000 to 59,000 ft)

MIDDLE

▲ *Altostratus* Tropics 2,000 to 8,000 m (7,000 to 26,000 ft)

LOW

▲ *Cumulus* Tropics 0 to 2,000 m (0 to 7,000 ft)

HIGH

▲ *Cirrocumulus and Cirrus* Middle latitudes
5,000 to 13,000 m (16,000 to 43,000 ft)

HIGH

▲ *Cirrostratus* (above cumulus) High latitudes
3,000 to 8,000 m (10,000 to 26,000 ft)

MIDDLE

▲ *Altocumulus* Middle latitudes 2,000 to
7,000 m (7,000 to 23,000 ft)

MIDDLE

▲ *Nimbostratus* High latitudes 2,000 to
4,000 m (7,000 to 13,000 ft)

LOW

▲ *Stratus* Middle latitudes 0 to 2,000 m (0
to 7,000 ft)

LOW

▲ *Stratocumulus* High latitudes 0 to 2,000 m
(0 to 7,000 ft)

The terms 'stratus' – for layer cloud – and 'cumulus' – for lumpy cloud – are the basic building blocks for cloud names. In addition to these indicators of form, meteorologists recognise three different heights at which clouds occur – simply low, middle and high. Which level a particular cloud falls into depends on the height of its base above the surface. Examples are provided on pages 66–67.

So, low cloud can, for example, be stratus (a monotonous layer of cloud); stratocumulus (a sheet of cloud that has a subtle 'lumpy' form to it); cumulus (a shallow, bubble-topped cloud); or cumulonimbus (the tallest, or deepest, cumulus cloud from which a shower falls – indicated by the inclusion of 'nimbus' in its name).

The many varieties of cloud at middle levels are prefixed by 'alto' – altostratus and altocumulus, for example. In addition, nimbostratus occurs at middle levels, as a deep layer of precipitating cloud.

The highest level clouds are prefixed by 'cirro'. In contrast to the low and middle types, they are composed entirely of ice crystals. As well as cirrostratus and cirrocumulus, there are the elegantly striated 'cirrus' that can occur as patches or long fibrous elements, which don't fit either of the cumuliform or stratiform forms.

The birth of cumulus

Because pressure decreases with height in the atmosphere, any parcels (bubbles) or layers of air that ascend will expand gradually. This increase in volume causes the air within the rising bubble to cool.

Air not only rises, of course: it must also come down in places. In this event, the air sinks into steadily rising pressure. Under these conditions, the air is warmed. So long as the ascending or descending air is unsaturated (cloud-free), it will cool or warm respectively at the rate of 9.8°C per kilometre (5.5°F per 1,000 ft).

Imagine a summer's day when the air temperature is 25°C (77°F) and the dew-point 15°C (59°F). A bubble of cloud-free air pulls away from the strongly heated surface as a thermal (a plume of relatively warm air that ascends invisibly through a cooler environment). These rise because the localized heating will decrease the plume's density, making it buoyant relative

Depressions

Clouds are formed by moist air rising in bubbles. However, moist air also rises on a very much larger scale within lows, or depressions (see page 21). This occurs across many hundreds of thousands of square kilometres of the Earth's surface during the formation of a typical low. Therefore, depressions are cloud-laden, often with deep layer cloud that can produce widespread precipitation. As lows track across the Earth, the cloud is borne with them.

▶ *Growing cumulus cloud with cirrus clouds above.*

▼*Expansion and cooling of an ascending dry air (cloudless) 'bubble'. As the air bubble ascends it cools, leading eventually to the appearance of cloud droplets.*

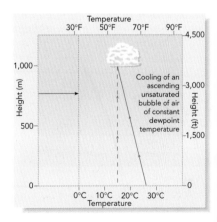

Dry Convection

During the day, air just above the Sahara Desert ascends in response to the intense heating of summer. It rises as vigorous thermals to a substantial height above the desert but generally is so dry that saturation is not achieved. This is known as dry convection.

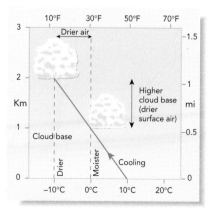

to the enveloping cooler, denser atmosphere. In this instance, the air is unsaturated so its temperature will decrease at a rate of 9.8°C per kilometre (5.5°F per 1,000 feet). If we assume that the concentration of water vapour remains constant as this happens – it can be increased if water is evaporated into the bubble and decreased if water condenses out of it – then after 100 m (330 ft) the temperature would be 24°C (75°F), which has a lower saturation value for water vapour than the air's surface temperature does.

Continued ascent will lead to further cooling of the bubble and therefore a gradual lowering of the saturation value, until, at 1,000 m (3,300 ft), the air will have cooled to its dewpoint temperature of 15°C (59°F). If the air ascends beyond that point, additional cooling will lead to the appearance of cloud droplets, formed from some water vapour in the bubble. This is where the cloudbase would be.

◀ *Influence of surface humidity*
on cumulus cloudbase.

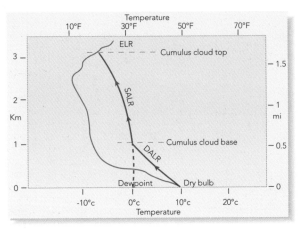

◀ **The parcel curve** (red) for cumulus cloud developing within a cooler environment (blue).

DALR: Dry Adiabatic Lapse Rate
ELR: Environmental Lapse Rate
SALR: Saturated Adiabatic Lapse Rate

Once the condensation begins, a cloud appears. The type associated with the thermal described above is a cumulus cloud. The process of condensation actually releases heat, which warms the surrounding air. This means that ascent within cloud causes the air to cool much more slowly than in cloud-free ascent.

The scattered cumulus have a clear subcloud layer, where the unsaturated bubbles are ascending, and a cloudbase that marks the level at which they become saturated. The height of the cloudbase depends on the temperature and dewpoint of the surface air. If the air is dry, it needs to ascend a considerable distance to produce condensation. If it is

▼ **Cumulus cloud streets**. Cloud streets appear when there is a temperature inversion with a constant wind. The clouds align themselves in the direction of the wind.

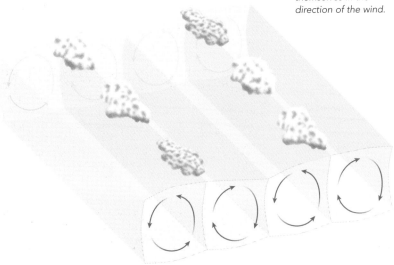

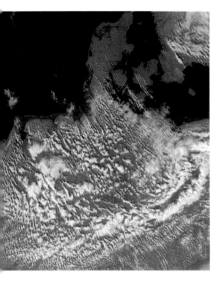

▲ **Visible satellite image** of cloud streets from Belgium to Poland on a March day.

moist, the cloudbase will be nearer the surface of the Earth.

The height to which a cumulus cloud grows depends partly on the moisture content of the bubble – that is, how much heating is available from condensation and, therefore, how buoyant it will be. This is determined by the dewpoint temperature: the higher the value, the greater the absolute concentration of moisture.

The thickness of the cloud is also affected by the way in which the temperature of the surrounding environment changes with height – known as the **environmental lapse rate**. The environmental lapse rate is sensed by weather balloons as they ascend through the troposphere and lower stratosphere. To estimate the potential depth of a cumulus cloud, it is necessary to compare the environment temperature curve to that of the thermal.

At any one time, it is possible to observe cumulus clouds of varying depth scattered over areas a few hundred kilometres across (up to 200 miles). Such differences may be related to changes in the intensity of surface heating, or to the way in which the environmental lapse rate varies from place to place.

Cloud streets

Some days, conditions can be such that convective clouds (see page 66) develop into a distinct pattern of long lines, separated by clear air. These lines may stretch for many tens or hundreds of kilometres along the direction of the wind and are known as cloud streets. They are formed when there is a temperature inversion (a rise in temperature with height)

► *A characteristically anvil-shaped* cumulonimbus. The flat top signifies that the upward-rushing air in the cloud has reached the stable lid of the troposphere, and the cloud\s ice crystals are then drawn out by the strong winds at upper levels. (See page 73)

a few kilometres above the surface, and when the wind direction remains constant with height below this level, with a speed of at least 13 knots at the surface. The cloud streets align along the average direction of the wind and, typically, are spaced about 10 km (6 mi) apart.

Since the streets occur when an inversion is present, the clouds do not usually become deep enough to produce any precipitation. They characterize pleasant, partly sunny weather, and last until larger-scale weather conditions change. Cloud streets are common over mid- and high-latitude oceans in the autumn and winter, and over the land in spring and summer.

▲ *Haboob or duststorm.* The cold downdraught produced by evaporative cooling inside the cloud spreads sideways and in arid areas, picking up dust.

▶ *Longer-lived cumulonimbus* where there is significant wind change with height.

▼ *Short-lived cumulus* where there is small/ no wind change with height.

Cumulonimbus

At the other extreme of the cumulus scale lie troposphere-deep cumulonimbus clouds, which are defined as low cloud because they have a base below 2,000 m (6,600 ft). These are the tallest clouds we see; because the depth of the troposphere increases from pole to equator, they can reach up to 20 km (12 mi) in low latitudes but only about 6 or 7 km (4 mi) in polar areas.

Since surface heating plays an important role in forcing the ascent of air from low levels, cumulonimbus clouds occur more frequently across strongly heated areas above which relatively cooler and/or drier air occurs, so the environmental lapse rate ensures that bubbles of air ascend to great heights. Unlike shallow cumulus, cumulonimbus clouds produce heavy rain and sometimes hail, thunder and lightning.

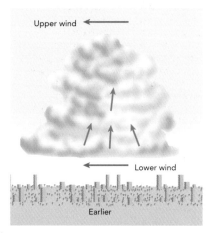

Upper wind ←

Lower wind →

Earlier

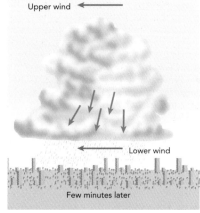

Upper wind ←

Lower wind →

Few minutes later

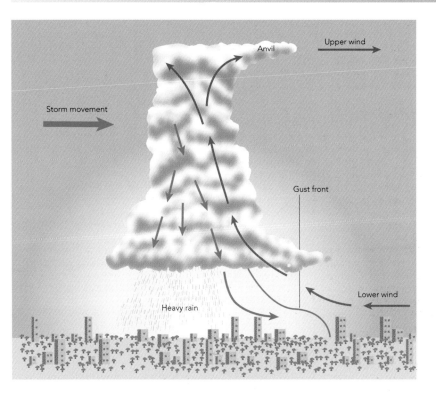

As the cloud grows rapidly up through the troposphere, it is vital that the updraught, which forms the core of the ascending air, is separated from any precipitation that starts to develop within the cloud. If this does not happen, any precipitation that forms will fall through the cloud-producing updraught, evaporating as it goes. This evaporating rain cools the air around it as it descends, which results in a cool sinking downdraught in the very core of the cloud. Thus, if a convective cloud grows in an environment where the wind speed and direction do not change with height, the cloud- and precipitation-producing ascent is 'killed' once the rain-drops fall back through it. Cumulus of this type commit suicide, producing only light showers in their short lifetime of a few tens of minutes.

If, however, the wind direction and speed do change with height, there is a chance that the updraught will be separated from the precipitation produced within the cloud. This is the recipe for a longer-lived, deep convective cloud that produces heavy, but generally short-lived, rain.

The region of the cloud where the rain occurs still experi-ences a downdraught produced by evaporative cooling,

Gust Fronts
Gust fronts are particularly dangerous to aircraft landing and taking off, because they can sweep across an airport some distance from the cloud in which they formed. Since aircraft take off and land into the wind, any sudden change of wind speed and direction can have fatal consequences.

and this feature can be dangerous. When it reaches the surface, it spreads quite rapidly sideways as a cool, and often very hazardous, gust front. In hot, arid areas, a gust front, and the air following it, may be made obvious if it becomes heavily dust-laden, suddenly cutting visibility to zero, as in the case of the haboobs of North Africa.

OROGRAPHIC ENHANCEMENT

Air has no choice but to flow over and around upland areas. If the air is damp, its forced ascent (termed orographic uplift) can often lead to saturation and condensation into orographic cloud. Such cloud is commonly thick stratus with a base below the tops of the hills over which the damp air flows. This situation produces hill fog for upland areas shrouded in such cloud – hilly areas are often cloudier than adjacent lower land because of the orographic effect. The amount of uplift required depends on how close the air is to saturation point. Very dry air will require a good deal of cooling (uplift) to reach its dewpoint temperature, while very damp air will need only slight ascent to produce cloud.

Within warm sectors of a weather front, rain is commonly subjected to a process known as orographic enhancement. Upland regions of South Wales in the UK, for example, can experience a fall of rain that is two or three times more intense than that falling on the coast at the same time. Careful study of this phenomenon has defined the conditions required to produce significantly heavier rain in upland areas – it is not true that a moist airstream crossing a hilly district will always generate more rain.

Orographic enhancement occurs in warm sectors when there is a precipitating layer of cloud at a height of

▶ *Role of low-level humidity in presence of orographic cloud. The low level flow must be damp enough (high enough dewpoint) to lead to condensation.*

▼ *Ingredients of heavier rain over hills (orographic enhancement). The strong, moist air at low-levels is a critical ingredient in maintaining the 'feeder' cloud over the hills. The rain from the higher 'seeder' cloud washes out a lot of cloud droplets from the feeder one – to produce the higher totals over hills. The feeder cloud must therefore receive a constant supply from the strong, damp, low level wind.*

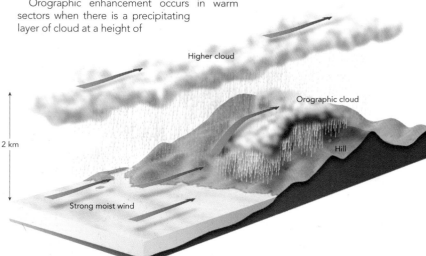

Higher cloud

Orographic cloud

2 km

Hill

Strong moist wind

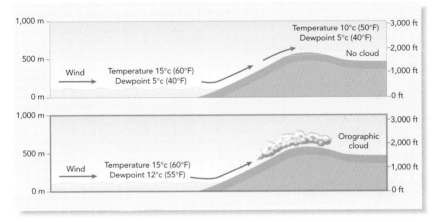

Temperature 10°c (50°F)
Dewpoint 5°c (40°F)
No cloud

Wind
Temperature 15°c (60°F)
Dewpoint 5°c (40°F)

Orographic cloud

Wind
Temperature 15°c (60°F)
Dewpoint 12°c (55°F)

▼ **Orographic higher level** *cloud streaming away northeastwards from the French Pyrenees.*

about 2 to 3 km (1 to 2 mi). This layer will not be related to the hills in any way, but to the large-scale flow of the frontal depression. Sometimes, as this layer moves across the hills, the rain it produces falls through cloud that has been generated by a strong, low-level stream of moist air flowing up and over the hills, visible as orographic cloud.

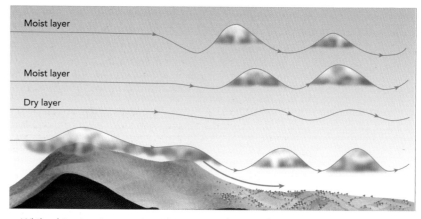

Moist layer

Moist layer

Dry layer

While this situation persists, the rain washes out large quantities of water from the lower cloud, thus increasing rainfall over the hills compared to other areas. If the lower cloud is constantly replenished by a strong surface flow of damp air, there will be a prolonged period (over many hours) of orographic enhancement. However, if the surface flow is weak, the water will soon be washed from the cloud, and not replenished at a rapid enough rate, providing only a fleeting addition to the catch over the hills.

▲ *Generation of lee wave clouds over high hill-sides or mountain ranges.*

This action occurs across many middle-latitude hilly areas that are frequented by frontal depressions. It is the explanation, for example, for the wet reputation of upland North Wales, Western Scotland and the Lake District in the UK. Other upland areas of the world that lie in the track of frontal cyclones also see orographic rain and snow. These include the Norwegian mountains, the Rockies of northwestern USA and western Canada, the southern Andes and the mountains of South Island, New Zealand. The winter season pressure maps in Chapter 2 illustrate the presence of such travelling lows in these regions.

Lee waves

Under special conditions of wind and temperature change with height, hills and mountains can generate standing waves, anchored to the hills and mountains that produce them, in the airflow above and downwind of them. These lee waves are indicated by cloud in the ascending air, contrasting with clear areas where the air descends. Such waves can appear over a distance of 100 km (60 mi) or more, to leeward of upland areas.

Lee waves can be compared to the standing waves sometimes seen in streams where water flows over large stones. The flow creates a pattern downstream, in which the waves are stationary, but the water flows quickly through the pattern.

The ribbed cloud pattern associated with lee waves will exist for some hours, rather than days, until the large-scale weather pattern that favours their development changes. The lenticular (lens-like) clouds produced by the wave pattern do not produce precipitation.

On some occasions, the droplets that compose the lee wave clouds freeze and, if the air is humid enough, an extensive sheet of ice crystals develops, which will be carried many kilometres/miles downstream by the wind. The true extent of such orographic cirrus can be seen from satellite photographs (see below).

PRECIPITATION

For precipitation to occur, there must be a means by which cloud droplets or ice crystals can grow larger and heavy enough to fall as drizzle, rain, snow or hail.

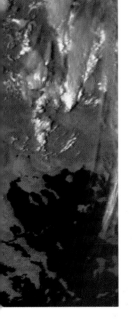

▼ *Satellite image of lee wave clouds over Italy, Albania, The Former Yugoslav Republic of Macedonia and Kosovo (seen as north-south aligned 'ribbed' clouds).*

Mares' Tails Cirrus

Evaporating precipitation can also be seen as the trailing component of 'Mares' tails' cirrus cloud, although the fact that the precipitation consists of ice crystals rather than raindrops is not obvious from the ground. This type of cloud occurs within a layer where the wind speed increases with height. The top part of the cloud is the source of the precipitating crystals, which fall through this zone to produce a trail that moves slowest at the base and quickest at the top.

Rain

Clouds with tops warmer than −15°C (5°F) are composed of cloud droplets of varying size, which collide as they settle. The larger drops fall faster and sweep up smaller drops by a process known as coalescence. The number of raindrops that form within these clouds depends on the liquid water content, the range of droplet sizes, the strength of the updraught within the cloud – which determines the time available for a droplet to grow – and even the electrical charge carried by the droplets.

If, by some process, cloud drops grow large enough to attain a fallspeed greater than the ascending air speed, they will fall as rain. A borderline cloud/drizzledrop has a diameter of about 0.2 mm, while a typical raindrop has a diameter of about 2 mm (0.07 in); a raindrop of this size falls at up to 6.5 m/sec (21 ft/sec). Drizzle is formed of drops with a diameter of between 0.2 and 0.5 mm.

Drizzle falls from shallow stratus, within which weak upcurrents of some 10 cm/sec (4 in/sec) occur, while vigorous tropical cumulus cloud will generate updraughts of many metres a second to produce raindrops of up to 5 mm (0.2 in) in diameter.

Even when drops do become large enough to fall out of the cloud, they suffer some evaporation in the subcloud layer, between the cloudbase and the surface. If the air in this layer is dry and the raindrops small, they may completely evaporate on their way down.

Sometimes it is possible to observe this evaporation when a shaft of rain or snow can be seen falling from clouds. The shaft will narrow towards the ground surface, vanishing above it. Such features are called virgae or fallstreaks (*see* photo, above).

▲ *Precipitation falling from cumulus clouds but not reaching the surface. If the rain drops are quite small and the air is dry, then they may evaporate before hitting the ground.*

ICE CRYSTAL FORMATION

Temperature	Basic form	Type of crystal
0°C to –4°C (32°F to 25°F)	plate	thin hexagons
–4°C to –10°C (25°F to 14°F)	prism	needle (–4°C to –6°C, 25°F to 21°F)
		hollow column (–5°C to –10°C, 23°F to 14°F)
–10°C to –22°C (14°F to –8°F)	plate	sector plate (–10°C to –12°C, 14°F to 10°F)
		dendrite (–12°C to –16°C, 10°F to 3°F)
		sector plate (–16°C to –22°C, 3°F to –8°F)
–22°C to –50°C (–32°F to –58°F)	prism	hollow column

Plate

Column

Dendrite

▲ *Microscopic image of a dendrite snow crystal. Above are three common forms of ice crystal. The shape an ice crystal takes depends on the temperature at which they are formed (see table, above).*

Snow

Under normal conditions, water freezes at 0°C (32°F). However, in the atmosphere, where water particles exist as extremely small cloud droplets, this is far from the case. Even at high altitudes within the troposphere, many cloud particles remain liquid in what is termed a supercooled state. Except at very low temperatures, liquid water will not freeze unless minute impurities are present. These are much less likely to occur in the very small droplets that form clouds than in substantial bodies of water where freezing occurs at 0°C (32°F). (Therefore, it is better to define 0°C (32°F) as the melting point of ice.)

In the atmosphere, only one cloud droplet in a million is frozen at –10°C (14°F), a couple of hundred or so in a million are frozen at –30°C (–22°F), and only at –40°C (–40°F) and below will they all be ice crystals.

Ice crystals that grow from vapour alone take on different characteristic shapes depending on the temperature range within which they are created. As they descend through progressively warmer layers, they become more complex in shape. Similarly complex form changes can occur if they

Winter Precipitation

Sleet is generally defined as snow that is melting as it settles on the surface, although in the USA the term is used for very cold raindrops that freeze into small ice pellets if they fall through a fairly deep layer of air just above the surface. **Freezing rain** occurs when raindrops fall from a higher, above-freezing region of air into a shallow sub-zero layer at the surface. The rain freezes on impact with all sorts of surfaces. During an **ice storm**, the accumulations of frozen rain (sometimes termed glaze) are so large that telephone lines come down, tree branches snap off and walking and driving are treacherous. An accumulation of a few cm of ice is fairly common in susceptible regions – over northeastern USA for example. They can reach some 30 cm (12 in) in extreme cases.

ascend on updraughts into cooler regions of a cloud. The table on the previous page summarizes the forms of these crystals.

The freezing of super-cooled water on to ice crystals is a second mechanism of growth. It is known as riming, which is essentially the same process that causes the deposit of rime as a frost (see page 89). The most effective surface to freeze water upon is an ice crystal, so if supercooled droplets touch one, they freeze instantly. This means that in clouds where both supercooled droplets and ice crystals are present, the crystals grow rapidly. Crystals may grow at varying rates depending on how much super-cooled water freezes on to them, and larger ones can capture others as they fall at higher speeds.

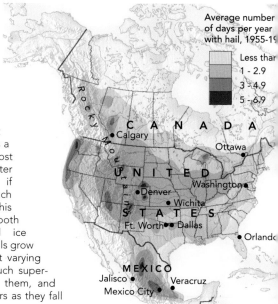

Average number of days per year with hail, 1955-19

Less than
1 - 2.9
3 - 4.9
5 - 6.9

The icy particles formed in this manner are known as graupel, which fall and fracture when they crash into cloud droplets. Such splinters can grow into new graupel, which may fragment again to produce a chain reaction, forming very large numbers of ice crystals. As these descend, they often stick together to produce snowflakes. In fact, most of the rain in middle and higher latitudes starts life as snow, even in the summertime.

Perhaps surprisingly, the heaviest snowfalls do not occur in the coldest air. Deep accumulations anywhere in the world are associated with moisture-rich air that has usually come across relatively warm seas. This is because the air must be relatively warm in order to contain large amounts of water vapour.

In middle and high latitude areas, the most common mechanism for producing substantial snowfalls is the frontal low (see page 40) – across the Rockies, the Andes and the European and New Zealand Alps, for example. Widespread, deep accumulations are often associated with air that streams through a depression's warm sector, although temperatures must be sub-zero right down to the surface.

Hail

Hail comprises of large pieces of ice that form within, and fall from, a cumulonimbus cloud. Such deep convective clouds are characterized by strong updraughts and downdraughts.

◄ The average number of days per year with hail, across North America, 1955–95. During the spring and summer months in particular there may be more than one hailstorm in a day.

The hailstones grow from graupel (ice crystals), which act as a nucleus, becoming larger due to the accumulation of supercooled water droplets as they are borne upwards on the rapidly ascending air. It is not uncommon for golfball-size hail to occur in the United States during the summer. Such hailstones probably will have been up and down through the same cloud a few times – over the course of ten minutes or so – before they acquire sufficient layers of ice to be heavy enough to fall out of the cloud and on to the surface. It is possible to count the number of ice layers in a large hailstone and thus gain an idea of the number of ascents it has made in the water-rich updraught.

It may seem paradoxical that we see such cold, icy objects in the warmest season; it's because convective clouds reach their greatest (and coldest) elevations when the surface is most strongly heated (in the summer), and they are most moisture-laden when evaporation rates are highest (also in the summer).

Thunder and lightning

Lightning is a massive electrical discharge between one cloud and another, from a cloud into the air, or between a cloud and the ground, and thunder is the audible component of the process. These two always go hand in hand.

Meteorologists do not agree on the way in which electric charge becomes separated within thunderclouds. The leading theory is that when hail and graupel fall through a layer of

▼ *Lightning develops in the cloud, creating an invisible stepped 'leader'.*

▼ *The upward positive current leaves the ground (usually from a tall object like a tree)*

▼ *The two currents meet, creating a channel which is used by a return stroke.*

Stepped leader

Return stroke

Measuring Storm Distance

The light from lightning reaches our eyes instantaneously, but the sound of thunder emanates from it at about 330 m/sec (1,000 ft/sec). This forms the basis for a rule that we can use to estimate our distance from the ground stroke. Count the seconds between the flash and the thunder – every second indicates a distance of about 330 m (1,000 ft). Therefore, a pause of three seconds means that the lightning hit about 1 km (0.6 mi) away. This rule holds good for distances of up to 5 km (3 mi); beyond that, we do not often hear thunder, because the sound is absorbed and refracted by the air.

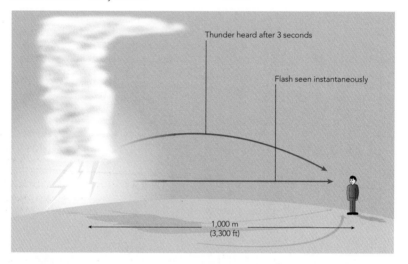

Thunder heard after 3 seconds

Flash seen instantaneously

1,000 m
(3,300 ft)

supercooled water and ice crystals that form the cloud, there is a transfer of positive charge from the slightly warmer hail to the colder cloud particles. The larger hail becomes negatively charged, accumulating such charge in the lower layers of the cloud. Conversely, the water and ice crystals gain positive charge and tend to accumulate in the upper reaches of the cloud on the updraught.

As the lower negative charge grows with the evolution of the cloud, it induces a region of positive charge below it on the surface, which moves along beneath the drifting cloud. This positive charge tends to be concentrated on objects that protrude from the surface and that are relatively isolated. Although dry air is quite a good electrical insulator, the potential difference that will grow under the right conditions is so enormous that a massive discharge is unavoidable. A difference of about 1,000,000 volts/m (300,000 volts/ft) is typical and will lead to a current of up to 100,000 amperes.

Lightning that reaches the ground first develops within the cloud, where electrons move rapidly down towards the base of the cloud, but in a stepped fashion. Every discharge runs for 100 m (330 ft) or so, then halts for about 50 millionths of a second before continuing downwards. This process is continued as an invisible stepped 'leader' until, near the ground, the potential gradient is so large that an upward positive current leaves the surface from tall objects such as trees and buildings. Once these two currents meet, electrons flow down to establish a channel that is used by a larger return stroke. This massive, brilliant upcurrent is what we see, and it lasts typically for about one ten-thousandths of a second.

Only about one in five lightning strokes are from cloud to ground. Each instantly heats the channel of air through which it flows by about 30,000°C (54,000°F). This means that the air expands incredibly quickly and very dramatically to produce a shock wave, which travels away from the lightning stroke at the speed of sound.

Rainbows

Sometimes, when the weather is showery, we see rainbows. These are visible when the Sun shines upon the falling drops – and it must be shining from behind us as we look towards the shower. This means, broadly, that in the morning, rainbows will be visible in the west, and in the afternoon, in the east.

When sunlight enters a raindrop, some of it passes straight through, while the remainder is reflected back by the rear surface of the drop. The angle at which

▲ *Primary (left) and faint secondary (right)* rainbows. *The secondary rainbow forms when light enters the raindrop at an angle so that double refraction occurs.*

▶ *Refraction and internal reflection of white light shining onto a raindrop. The refracted light appears in the sky as a striking, multi-coloured rainbow.*

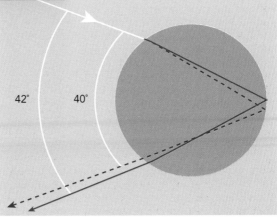

Gauging Humidity

One way of determining whether cloud-free air is relatively dry or moist is to watch the stars. If they twinkle, humidity in the air is refracting the light coming from them; if they do not twinkle, the troposphere is quite dry.

this occurs is about 42 degrees; as the light enters the raindrop, each ray is refracted slightly differently, as is each ray leaving the drop. When combined with the internal reflection, this double refraction splits the 'white' sunlight that shines on to a drop into its component colours, in the same way that a prism splits white light into the colours of the spectrum.

When this happens within a mass of falling raindrops, we see a rainbow. Refracted red light enters our eyes from higher drops, and violet light from lower drops. As a result, the brilliant rainbow we see is red at the top and violet at the bottom. Occasionally, there may be a fainter, but noticeable, secondary rainbow. This forms when sunlight enters the raindrops at such an angle that a double internal reflection occurs. As a result, the light that finally leaves such drops is fainter and the colours weaker.

FOG

Fog is defined as a condition where the horizontal visibility is 1,000 m (3,300 ft) or less because of the presence of water droplets suspended in the atmosphere. Thick fog is defined as having visibility of 100 m (c.300 ft) or less. Impaired visibility of more than 1,000 m (3,000 ft) is defined as mist.

Inland on a cloudless, calm night when the air has low humidity, there will be a large flow of radiation from the Earth's surface and atmosphere out into space. If cloud is present, its

▼ **Surface chilling at night** in dry atmospheres. In very cold conditions, in a very dry atmosphere, there is a strong radiative cooling to space.

Evolution of radiation fog during the night

At sunset, in clear, calm conditions, radiative cooling occurs up through damp air.

A few hours later, radiative cooling continues and fog occurs at the surface.

The fog deepens, as the radiative cooling continues under clear conditions.

water vapour, water droplets and ice crystals will absorb some of this outgoing energy and radiate some of it back down to the surface and lower levels of the atmosphere. Therefore, cloud – especially layer cloud – acts like an insulator.

If the sky is cloud-free, but the air is humid, the water vapour present will also absorb some of the outgoing radiation and, like a cloud layer, will radiate some of it back to the surface and lower layers, keeping them warmer than they would be otherwise. If, however, the air has very low humidity, much of the heat will escape to space, and the surface will be much chillier.

Once the Sun is low in the sky and the air begins to cool, it does so most strongly at the surface. Thus, the chilling tends to be most marked at and near the ground, notably on calm nights. This means that a temperature inversion will form above the surface, in which the temperature increases with height. If the conditions are calm, or near calm, the air adjacent to the surface may cool until it reaches its dewpoint. Light, subtle movement will spread the cooling through the surface layer; any stronger motion – if the wind picks up – will mix the warmer air above and the chilly layer below, destroying the conditions that favour fog formation.

◄ **Surface chilling at night** in humid atmospheres. In cold/cool conditions, when there is some water vapour, but it is cloud-free, the cooling to space is offset by re-radiation downwards.

Radiation fog

Calm, cloud-free conditions can produce radiation fog. The word 'radiation' expresses the means by which the air is cooled to its dewpoint temperature – the Earth and the atmosphere lose heat rapidly by radiating it to space.

Once the fog develops and grows vertically, the effective radiating surface is no longer the ground, but the top of the fog. The temperature inversion is found at the top, too, often many metres above the ground.

Radiation fog is most common when chilling is strongest, during the autumn and winter, and it is confined to land areas. Its frequency depends on the distance from the sea and the local lie of the land. Such fog tends to occur more frequently across low-lying areas, like valleys, into which cool air drains slowly during the hours of darkness.

The sea cools only marginally at night – considerably less than the land surface does. In fact, marine cooling is so minimal that it does not lead to radiation fog.

▲ *Radiation fog* in *the valley around Neuschwanstein Castle, Germany. The cold air has moved slowly down the mountain valleys to produce fog in the lower land surrounding the castle.*

Advection fog

Cooling of the air can also occur when a warm air mass flows across a colder surface, in which case heat is transferred downwards from the air. This can reduce the air temperature to its dewpoint, producing saturation, then fog. The critical difference between advection fog and radiation fog is the role played by air movement in its formation. The term 'advection' is used almost exclusively in meteorology and oceanography, normally referring to horizontal motion that transports some property of the fluid. For example, 'thermal

▲ **Relatively warm, moist air** from the southwest is strongly chilled as it flows across the cooler waters between Denmark and Sweden.

◄ **Advection fog** lapping the Californian coast, USA. Warm and moist air has crossed the cool Californian Ocean Current and been chilled sufficiently to produce a typical advection (or sea) fog.

advection' refers to the amount of heat transported by the wind or ocean currents.

Advection fog is commonly found in areas of poleward-moving tropical maritime air that is cooled by contact with the sea's surface. Thus, it is also known as sea fog. It occurs most often in the spring and early summer, when the sea's surface temperature is at, or recovering from its lowest.

Persistently cool areas of ocean witness more frequent advection fog, although it is not very common within the tropics. Among these regions are the Grand Banks, off Newfoundland, where, in July, advection fog occurs on four out of ten days over the cool waters of the Labrador current. It is as common over the cool Oya Shio and Kamchatka waters in the northwest Pacific, and in the Bering Strait. In higher latitudes, sea fog is frequently found over the pack ice and open waters of the summertime Arctic Ocean and Canadian archipelago, and to some extent over the pack ice and open waters around Antarctica.

Coastal advection fog often occurs where unusually cold sea water flows parallel to subtropical western continents. Strong cooling of the low-level air leads to fog along the coast of northwest Africa (over the Canaries Current), southwest Africa (the Benguela Current), Chile (the Humboldt Current) and, perhaps most famously, the central and northern California coast. In the seas around Britain, especially to the southwest from where the tropical maritime air most often approaches, advection fog is also common. On Britain's east coast, too, the cooling of moist onshore flow

◄ Hill fog occurs when layer cloud intersects the tops of the hills.

leads to the development of the 'fret' along the Northumbrian coast and 'haar' across the coast of eastern Scotland.

By definition, advection fog moves. This means that even with winds of 30 knots over the sea, thick fog may still be present. However, with strengthening wind, the fog often lifts to form extensive stratiform cloud.

Although advection fog is most common over the sea, it can occur over land when warm, moist air passes across a snow-covered surface or one that has recently been frosty.

Hill fog

Another frequent type of fog is hill fog, which occurs when layer cloud intersects a range of hills, reducing visibility in those portions of the hills within the cloud to 1 km (half a mile) or less. Hill fog often occurs in moist warm sectors of frontal depressions, where the cloud base is low

▼ Arctic sea smoke or 'steam fog'. Arctic sea smoke is formed when very cold air comes in contact with a comparatively warm body of water.

Arctic sea smoke

Occasionally, when cold air spills over much warmer water, the extreme temperature gradient through the air just above the water triggers very localized rapid ascent of bubbles of air, within which the water vapour condenses as narrow plumes. These features are known as Arctic sea smoke or steam fog. They can occur over open water in the Arctic and over lakes in middle latitudes in the winter.

Dew

Dew forms by the direct condensation of water vapour on to the ground, most noticeably on grass. Dew will occur under conditions that favour the generation of radiation fog. It is deposited before such fog develops, but is often observed when there is no fog at all. On these occasions, the cooling is sufficient to produce a dewfall, but is not intense enough to affect condensation within the lowest layers of the atmosphere. In regions where precipitation is generally sparse, dew can provide an important source of water, for both plants and animals.

Frost

The most common form of frost is hoar frost. It is the equivalent of dew, but the water vapour is deposited as ice crystals in the form of scales, needles, feathers, etc. on blades of grass, bushes and other surfaces. Like dew, hoar frost develops under clear, calm conditions. The temperature to which the air must cool to produce frost is not the dewpoint, but the frost-point. This is defined as the temperature to which the air must be cooled (at fixed pressure) to saturate it with respect to an ice surface, rather than a liquid water surface.

A less common form of frost, which often produces dramatic forms, is rime. This occurs when supercooled cloud and fog droplets come into contact with cold surfaces to form masses of white ice crystals. Rime is most commonly found in upland areas during winter. Sometimes, amazing shapes may be observed because the crystals are deposited while the supercooled cloud or hill fog is in motion. The frost formation grows downstream of the object on which the deposit was first made.

Visible frost does not always occur when the air temperature falls below 0°C (32°F). Sometimes the air is so dry that overnight chilling is not intense enough to squeeze any water out of the air as a deposit of frost. Nevertheless, if the surface temperature reaches or falls below 0°C (32°F), ground frost is reported.

▲ *Thick hoar frost* deposited on leaves and exposed roots.

▼ *Rime frost*, Snowdon, Wales, UK. The ice crystals are deposited by cold, cloudy air flow.

Operational meteorology relies upon a wide range of observations for the analysis of the current global weather situation and the prediction of its evolution over hours and days. To forecast, it is essential that the current state of the atmosphere is known, not only at the surface, but also throughout its depth. Observations around the world must be taken simultaneously, using the Universal Time Co-ordinated (UTC or GMT) clock, so that weather centres have a 'snapshot' or synoptic view of the global, regional and local weather.

The measurements that are taken routinely at weather stations across the globe are a standard set of observations laid down by international agreement through the agency of the United Nations' World Meteorological Organization (WMO) in Geneva, Switzerland. The WMO also sponsors and co-ordinates some observational weather and climate programmes that improve the understanding of, for example, atmospheric processes on scales that range from a small cluster of clouds to that of an almost global scale. It is also a major sponsor of meteorological training across a range of levels, partly through its world-wide system of Regional Meteorological Training Centres.

Surface weather is observed operationally on an hourly basis at busy airports and military airfields. At many other sites, however, observations are only taken every three, six or perhaps 12 hours. In these cases, it is important that they include the hours of 0000 and 1200 UTC, because these are the key times on which many forecasts are based. There is a significant trend in many weather services to automate all, or many, of the tasks traditionally carried out by members of staff. Doubtless, this will continue, leading to a decline in the availability of, for example, information on visibility and cloud type and the amount of data that are currently impractical and/or too expensive to assess automatically.

Normally, the surface observations reported every hour are:

- dry bulb temperature
- dewpoint temperature
- mean-sea-level barometric pressure
- pressure tendency
- total cloud amount
- cloud type and base height
- horizontal visibility
- wind direction and speed
- present and past weather
- precipitation total (usually 12- or 24-hour)

To an observer, the term 'weather' does not mean simply 'dry and sunny' or 'wet and windy'. It means something much more specific, related to prevailing conditions at the time of the observation. An observer must choose one of a hundred possibilities to report; something must be occurring, even if it is as apparently innocuous as 'clouds developing during past hour'. Present weather types each have a distinct

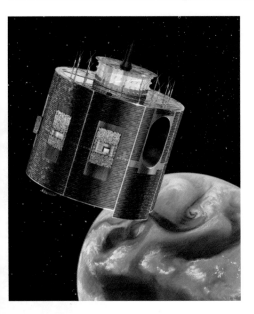

▲ *Meteosat 8, the first of the new Meteosat Second Generation (MSG) satellites, will deliver some twenty times as much information as its predecessor Meteosats. It images every 15 minutes rather than 30 and has much-improved spatial resolution.*

two-digit number from 00 to 99 ranked so that, broadly, the more 'significant' the weather, the larger the number allotted to it (*see* page 114).

Past weather must also be reported. Observers may select two broad weather types from a list of ten. The period during which this factor is reported depends on the hour of observation. Those made at 0000, 0600, 1200 and 1800 UTC relate to the previous six hours, for example.

Surface observations are then supplemented by information collected by other means. Over the last 50 years or so, global upper-air observations have developed into an essential component of the network, providing all-important information on how temperature, humidity, wind direction and speed vary up to about 20 km (12 mi) above sea level. These variables are monitored by balloon-borne instrument packages called radiosondes, which are released routinely four times a day – usually at 0000, 0600, 1200 and 1800 UTC. Wind data are available at each of these hours, whereas temperature and humidity are usually recorded only at 0000 and 1200 UTC. Although there are many fewer upper-air stations than surface sites worldwide, the data are crucially important to the individual forecaster and to computer-based global weather prediction schemes.

There are currently only a few ocean weather ships remaining. These are dedicated to measuring surface conditions every hour and release radiosondes four times a day. They steam around fixed locations in the central and eastern North Atlantic, but are being substituted nowadays by roving commercial ships. Such vessels release radiosondes automatically at the appropriate time, wherever they are. These ships have agreements with their national weather service, so that they fly the flag of whichever country they are from: the UK, Finland, Germany and the USA for example. Their weather balloon observations are transmitted automatically to major weather forecasting centres – usually via satellite.

Measuring the atmosphere is not confined to surface and upper-air observation stations. Since 1960, weather satellites have orbited the Earth (*see* pages 106–111), not only providing operational meteorologists with details of the location of clouds across the globe, but also with many other useful applications. These include vertical profiling of temperature and humidity levels throughout the atmosphere to help fill the large gaps in the radiosonde network.

Radar (see pages 104–106) has also evolved since World War 2 into a useful tool for weather analysis because it can be 'tuned' to sense precipitation within about 100 km (60 mi) of the antenna. Today, for example, Canada is covered by a network of such radars, from which a national map of the extent and intensity of precipitation is produced every 15 minutes (see pages 104–105). Many other weather services have similar systems. Precipitation radars across Australia have dual purpose in some areas where, generally, population is sparse. In such places, they are used for tracking balloons to produce estimates of wind speed and direction up through the atmosphere. The area covered by each radar is basically the same as those in Canada.

The national network of Doppler radars in the USA offers a complete cover by these more sophisticated instruments. They provide maps of precipitation and low level wind fields that indicate the location of convergence lines along which the air streams together as a possible harbinger of thunderstorms.

SURFACE MEASUREMENTS

A properly exposed weather screen will house a number of instruments. The screen is designed to ensure that the air temperature measured really is just that – the temperature of the air flowing through it via the gaps between its sides' downward-angled slats. The reflective quality of the box's white finish combines with its insulated floor and roof to minimize any effect on the air temperature by sunshine or the temperature of the ground below the screen. Many instruments routinely in use today were developed many decades ago. More modern electrical instruments are also used, by necessity, in automatic weather stations. There is, not surprisingly perhaps, a modern-day trend in many weather services to automate observations. This is true at sea as well as on land. Observations taken manually or automatically are transmitted electronically to regional sites then on to the national weather centre.

▼ *Dry bulb (left) and wet bulb (right)* thermometers in a weather screen. The dry bulb measures air temperature, the wet bulb thermometer measures humidity (see page 96).

Temperature

Air temperature is measured by using a mercury-in-glass thermometer that is

► *Horizontally-*
mounted maximum
(top) and minimum
thermometers,
thermograph (left) and
hygrograph (right) inside
a weather screen. The
thermometers measure
the highest and lowest
temperatures over a
particular time period
– usually 24 hours.

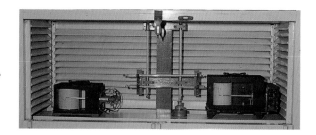

read to the nearest 0.1°C (0.1°F). This is known as a dry bulb thermometer.

Also housed within the screen are the horizontally-mounted maximum and minimum thermometers which are designed specifically to record the highest and lowest temperatures that occur during a specified time period, often 24 hours from 0900 local time. Commonly, the maximum occurs during the mid-afternoon, and the minimum during the hours of darkness. Occasionally, however, the timing is very different, particularly outside the tropics, when airmass changes occur in association with the moving passage of frontal depressions.

The maximum thermometer is a mercury-in-glass instrument with a constriction in the narrow central thread, near the bulb. The mercury can expand unimpeded from the bulb and through the constriction as the air temperature increases. Once the temperature falls, however, the length of the mercury thread is preserved because the fluid is prevented from returning to the bulb by the constriction. Thus the maximum temperature is recorded and will remain so until the instrument is reset in the same manner as a clinical thermometer, which records body temperature using the same principle.

The minimum thermometer contains alcohol rather than mercury because its lower freezing point (–114.4°C [156.1°F] compared to –38.9°C [–38.0°F]) makes it more useful in very cold regions. Alcohol expands along the thin bore of the instrument as the air temperature increases, and retreats when it cools. Suspended within the alcohol is a very thin 'index', or marker, which is dragged back along the bore by the alcohol's meniscus as the air temperature falls. As the air warms once more, the alcohol will expand along the bore, leaving the index behind, and the tip furthest from the bulb will mark the minimum temperature precisely. Usually, this type of thermometer is reset once a day by gently tilting it so that the index drifts back to the meniscus.

A forecast of 'tonight's low' or 'today's high' refers to the minimum measurement in a weather screen. In addition to this measurement, daily mimima are also recorded over grass, bare soil and concrete surfaces.

All the measurements described so far are 'point' values. In contrast, the thermograph, an old-fashioned, but still widely used instrument, provides a continuous trace of temperature, typically over a period of a week. Essentially, it consists of a pen on the end of a long arm attached to a bimetallic coil, which distorts as the air temperature rises and falls. The pen traces such fluctuations on a thermogram – a paper strip chart – wrapped around a clockwork-driven drum.

Pressure

To measure atmospheric pressure is to weigh the great mass of air that presses down upon the Earth. The pressure decreases with height through the atmosphere, because there is progressively less air above a given level. It's useful to measure because if it is analysed on a map by drawing isobars, forecasters can immediately see the location and intensity of weather-producing features.

This downward pressure can support a column of water, or other fluid, in a glass tube immersed in a reservoir at its lower open end, and topped by a vacuum at its upper sealed end. Atmospheric pressure is such that at sea level, this water column would be about 10 m (33 ft) high. The high density of mercury means that its column height is a more manageable 75 cm (30 in) or so.

The mercury barometer was developed during the 1640s by Evangelista Torricelli, a student of Galileo. It is still widely used, but its reading must be corrected for the influence of the surrounding air temperature and variations in the strength of gravity. Both affect the height of the mercury column.

The 'station level' pressure is read to the nearest 0.1 mbar (0.1 'hectopascal' or hPa), but this reading must be adjusted to a common datum, which is mean-sea-level. This entails adding a certain number of millibars to represent the pressure of an imaginary column of air between the barometer and mean-sea-level. If this was not done, the resulting weather chart would look like a topographical map. This is because the rapid change of pressure going up through the atmosphere (about 1 mbar every 10 m [33 ft] near sea level) would completely conceal the much more subtle change of pressure across the surface caused by genuine highs and lows (typically 1 mbar every 100 km [60 mi]). If a weather station is below sea level the adjustment is made by subtracting so many millibars from the reading.

Many homes have what are known as aneroid (without air) barometers. This type senses the pressure through small distortions of a partly evacuated metal capsule. Higher atmospheric pressure will 'squash' it more than lower pressure. The capsule is linked mechanically to the familiar arrow that moves around a scale of millimetres and/or inches

▲ *A mercury barometer.* *The height of the mercury column is a measure of atmospheric pressure. The air's pressure changes with the weather. Corrections must be made to the reading to allow for the influences of temperature and gravity.*

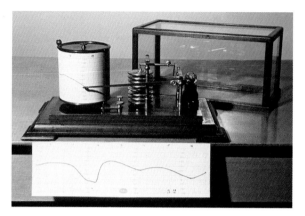

◀ *A barograph* with an example of a week's trace of the variations in atmospheric pressure. The barograph automatically records change in pressure on to paper.

▼ *Two examples of precipitation gauges.* The standard 5" rain gauge (top) and the graduated measuring vessel (bottom).

of mercury, and of millibars. In addition, the over-simplified, and often unreliable, forecasts of 'Dry', 'Change', 'Wet', etc. are printed on the face of the instrument alongside the scales.

The drawback of a barometer is that it provides only an indication of pressure at the time it is read, which is of limited use. More significant is the rate of change of pressure with time at each station and the pattern of pressure across the surface at mean-sea-level, because weather-producing features such as highs and lows are identified by its routine mapping.

The change of pressure with time is portrayed by a barograph, an aneroid instrument with an indicating arm that traces a continuous line of pressure on a barogram – a paper strip wrapped around a clockwork-driven drum. The barogram is usually changed once a week.

In addition to the 'spot' value of pressure, the barograph also provides its 'tendency', because it is very useful to know the size and direction (up or down) of a station's pressure change. Typically, this covers the three hours leading up to the observation time.

Precipitation

The term 'precipitation' encompasses all forms of water particle that fall from the atmosphere to the Earth's surface. In addition to rain, it also includes drizzle, snow and hail.

The most common instrument for measuring precipitation is a raingauge that is emptied once a day to provide a simple record of fall in millimetres or inches. The design varies little from country to country: often it comprises a 12.7 cm (5 in) diameter copper cylinder with its top 30.5 cm (12 in) above the surrounding surface. This height reduces the risk of water splashing in from the ground and aids the retention of snow.

Precipitation that falls into the gauge runs down a funnel with a narrow aperture to minimize evaporative losses. It is collected in a vessel (often a glass bottle) that is sunk into the ground. Once a day, the observer decants the water into a tapered glass measuring vessel to determine the amount to the nearest 0.1 mm (0.01 in).

Gauges should be sited well away from any objects, such as bushes or buildings, that may affect the natural trajectory of any precipitation. In a sense, all are 'active' instruments because their presence affects airflow and thus the drift of precipitation, which would fall differently if the gauges were not present.

Daily totals are useful, but do not provide information about the intensity and duration of precipitation, which is essential for detailed studies. Autographic or recording raingauges are designed to satisfy the requirement for such detail on a strip chart that is usually changed daily, or automatically as a telemetred radio message from the gauge to a central point. A common type is the 'tipping bucket' design, in which two small open metal containers on a see-saw mechanism are used to collect the precipitation. When one bucket is filled by the required amount, it tips, moving the other into position to continue collecting any further precipitation. The tipping action is registered on the strip chart trace.

HUMIDITY

The measurement of humidity that springs to mind for most people is that of relative humidity. In fact, this is one of its least useful definitions.

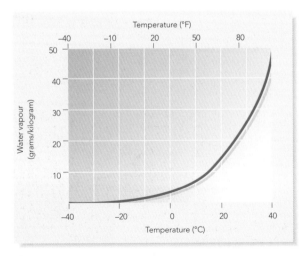

◄ *Graph showing saturation specific humidity* as a function of temperature. *The mass of water vapour in saturated air increases dramatically as temperature rises.*

Some of the definitions of humidity used in meteorology are listed below:

Absolute humidity The maximum amount of water vapour (in grams) that can be contained in a cubic metre of the air and water vapour mixture.

Specific humidity The mass of water vapour (in grams) in a kilogram of the air and water vapour mixture.

Mixing ratio The mass of water vapour (in grams) present in a kilogram of dry air.

Vapour pressure The pressure exerted at the Earth's surface by water vapour contained in the atmospheric column. This varies from virtually zero to about 3% of the total pressure, which is typically 1,000 mbar.

Relative humidity The ratio, expressed as a percentage, of the actual amount of water vapour contained in a sample of air to the amount it could contain if saturated at the observed dry bulb temperature.

Humidity is measured in weather screens by the wet bulb method. The bulb of a mercury-in-glass thermometer is snugly covered by a muslin bag that is kept permanently wet with distilled water supplied by a wick. Although the wet bulb temperature is read in degrees Celsius or Fahrenheit, in fact it is a measure of humidity (*see* page 92).

The wet-bulb temperature reading forms the basis of the calculations for both relative humidity and absolute humidity. The specific humidity of air that is saturated with water vapour increases with temperature. Saturated air with a temperature of 0°C (32°F) contains 3.0 g/kg; at 10°C (50°F) this rises to about 7.0 g/kg; at 20°C (68°F) it is about 14.0 g/kg; and at 30°C (86°F) it is 26.0 g/kg.

Let us assume that on a summer's day we record a dry-bulb temperature of 30°C (86°F) and a wet-bulb value of 15°C (59°F). The actual absolute humidity of this sample

▼ An example of a weekly hygrogram.
A hygrometer is used to measure the amount of moisture, or humidity, in the air. Changes in humidity are recorded on a hygrogram.

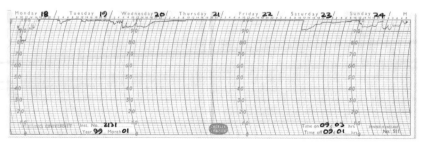

of air is deduced from the wet-bulb temperature, using standard hygrometric tables. These will also specify the value of absolute humidity if the air was saturated at its dry bulb temperature of 30°C (86°F).

In this case, the observed absolute humidity is 11 g/m^3, while the saturation (maximum possible) absolute humidity is 30 g/m^3. Therefore, the relative humidity is 11 g/m^3 ÷ 30 g/m^3 = 37%.

The same value of relative humidity can be obtained from very different samples of air scattered around the globe, so it is not of great use to meteorologists. They find absolute values of water vapour much more useful because these permit significant calculations to be made – for example, how much precipitation might fall from a column of air if all or some of the water vapour in it condenses.

In addition to the spot values of relative humidity provided by the dry- and wet-bulb thermometers in the screen, a time trace can also be provided by a recording hygrometer. These vary, but one type commonly in use is the hair hygrometer, which takes advantage of the fact that horse (and human) hair lengthens and shortens as relative humidity varies. Human hair shrinks in length by some 2.5% when relative humidity reduces from 100% to 0%.

A small sheaf of hair is stretched across a thin metal bar, which is connected mechanically to a pen that traces fluctuations in relative humidity on a hygrogram strip chart. This is wrapped around a rotating drum and normally is changed once a week.

Other hygrometers are based on the moisture-absorbing properties of various chemicals, which become moister as the humidity increases.

Cloud amount and type

By international agreement, cloud amount is reported as eighths (or oktas) of the sky covered, as both individual layers of cloud and as total cloud amount, which summarizes one or more types of cloud that may be present.

Clouds belong to one of three layers, defined simply as low, middle or high. The layer in which they occur depends on the height of their base above the surface: the definition of these three layers varies with latitude, such that the height limits generally increase with decreasing.

There is a very large variety of cloud types (*see* pages 66–67), which are separated into three primary groups. Each of the groups contains two or three principal cloud forms.

High clouds	Cirrus, cirrocumulus and cirrostratus
Middle clouds	Altocumulus, altostratus and nimbostratus
Low clouds	Stratus, stratocumulus, cumulus and cumulonimbus

▶ *An anemometer and wind vane.*
The exertion of the wind on the three hemispheric cups causes the supporting shaft to rotate in accordance with the wind speed. The speed is then displayed on a calibrated dial or digitally.

Cumulus clouds have a 'bubbly' appearance; cirrus clouds are wispy; stratus is sheet-like; and nimbus clouds are rain-bearing. These basic cloud types can be combined, hence cirrocumulus and nimbostratus, etc. The prefixes 'alto' and 'cirro' are applied specifically to middle and high clouds respectively.

Wind speed and direction

Wind speed is measured by using an anemometer. The type used routinely at weather stations is the cup anemometer, which usually has three hemispherical cups mounted on a vertical shaft. The pressure exerted by the wind on the concave inner faces of the cups is greater than that on their convex outer faces, which causes the vertical shaft to rotate. The rotation rate varies with the wind

Beaufort scale

In 1806, Francis Beaufort, a Royal Naval officer, developed a scale to express the effect of different wind speeds on the sea's surface. Later, information was added to facilitate the scale's use over land, and by the early 20th century, numerical values of wind speed had been linked to the Beaufort numbers 0 to 12.

BEAUFORT SCALE			
Force	Specifications for use on land	Equivalent mean wind speed 10 m (33 ft) above ground	
0	Calm; smoke rises vertically	0 kt	0 m s-1
1	Light air; wind direction shown by smoke drift, not by vanes	2	0.8
2	Light breeze; wind felt on face; leaves rustle; vanes move	5	2.4
3	Gentle breeze; leaves and small twigs moving; light flags lift	9	4.3
4	Moderate breeze; dust and loose paper lift; small branches move	13	6.7
5	Fresh breeze; small leafy trees sway; crested wavelets on lakes	19	9.3
6	Strong breeze; large branches sway; telegraph wires whistle; umbrellas difficult to use	24	12.3
7	Near gale; whole trees move; inconvenient to walk against	30	15.5
8	Gale; small twigs break off; impedes all walking	37	18.9
9	Strong gale; slight structural damage	44	22.6
10	Storm; seldom experienced on land; considerable structural damage; trees uprooted	52	26.4
11	Violent storm; rarely experienced; widespread damage	60	30.5
12	Hurricane; at sea, visibility is badly affected by driving foam and spray; sea surface completely white	>64	>32.7

speed, which is displayed on a calibrated dial marked with knots (nautical miles per hour), metres per second and other units. A properly exposed anemometer will be mounted 10 m (33 ft) above the surface.

In operational meteorology, the wind-speed anemometer measurements are averaged over the course of a few minutes. The value measured is the horizontal wind speed, and while the vertical component is important, it is not measured routinely – typically, it is about 100 times smaller than the horizontal wind. In some circumstances, however, it can actually outweigh the horizontal wind speed, as with the strong vertical currents associated with very deep cumulus clouds, for example.

Combined with the anemometer is a vane that points into the wind to show the direction from which it is blowing. Commonly, this consists of a horizontal arm with a pointer at one end and a streamlined vertical plate at the other. Movements of the vane are transmitted to an anemograph, which provides a continuous trace of direction fluctuations.

A wind direction report is usually given as an average taken over a few minutes, and it is expressed in degrees read clockwise from true north to the nearest ten degrees. The value of 000° is reserved for calm conditions when there is no wind. An easterly (that is, a wind blowing from the east) has a direction of 090°, a southerly blows from 180°, a westerly from 270°, and a northerly from 360°. There are finer gradations, such as a south-westerly being 225°.

The convention in meteorology is to report the direction from which the air flows because it is important to know its past trajectory. The temperature and humidity of the air are partly determined by the nature of the surfaces over which it approaches an observation site.

Sunshine

The routine method of measuring the duration of 'bright sunshine' is to use a sensitized card held in a frame wrapped around one half of a glass sphere that focuses the Sun's rays on to it. The term 'bright' indicates that this type of recorder is not sensitive enough to record sunshine around sunrise and sunset. It provides a

▶ *Radiation fog.*
The cooling of air near the earth's surface, usually at night, causes radiation fog. The fog is quite shallow and tends to disappear as the day warms up.

total duration of bright sunshine to the nearest tenth of an hour every day.

A more useful measurement is that of the intensity of solar radiation at the surface, expressed in Watts per square metre. Some observation sites use solarimeters to sense this variable, the most basic type using a device known as a thermopile, which converts heat into electrical energy.

The solar radiation takes two forms: direct and diffuse. The former reaches the instrument directly from the Sun, while the diffuse (or sky radiation) arrives after being scattered by gas molecules, dust and other particles.

◀ A Campbell-Stokes sunshine recorder.
The sunshine recorder is comprised of a clear glass sphere that focuses the sun's rays onto a sensitized chart. The rays produce a charred line when there is bright sunshine. The length of the line indicates the duration of bright sunshine.

◀ A solarimeter.
Solarimeters are used at weather stations to measure the intensity of surface solar radiation. Solar radiation falls onto a black thermopile that converts the incident energy into an electrical current that is then converted into radiance in Watts per square metre.

Visibility

Visibility is the distance at which an object can be seen and identified by someone with normal eyesight under normal daylight conditions. It is an indication of the air's opacity, and it depends on the nature of the particles in suspension. These range from extremely small particles of smoke, dust or water that settle out very slowly in light winds, to coarse particles that are kept in suspension only by the turbulence associated with strong winds. Duststorms, sandstorms and some blizzards fall into this latter category. The former is characterized by haze when the particles are dry, or mist and fog when water is present.

At synoptic stations, the observer must assess the poorest horizontal visibility (it may vary with direction from the vantage point used). At land stations, visibility is quoted to the nearest 100 m (about 330 ft) up to 5 km (about 3 mi), then to the nearest kilometre from 5 km to 30 km (about 19 mi), and every 5 km up to a maximum of 75 km (about 48 mi). This is achieved by reference to objects at specific distances from the vantage point. If visibility is extremely poor – a visibility of less than 100 m (330 ft) – it is reported to the nearest 10 m (about 33 ft).

Taking these measurements is particularly difficult at sea because there are no objects located at fixed distances from a ship. Therefore, the scale used for marine visibility observations is much coarser, as is that for climatological stations at which values are logged only once a day.

At night, reports are often based on unfocused lights of moderate intensity at known distances and, if appropriate, the silhouettes of hills or mountains against the sky.

Commonly, these values are assessed by eye. However, there are automatic visibility meters that measure the change in intensity of a beam over a short distance, which is then extrapolated to provide an estimate of visibility that is consistent with the routine method.

MARINE OBSERVATIONS

In addition to reporting on visibility, ships also report sea-surface temperature and the speed and direction of their motion. The reason for this is that pressure tendencies reported by them are not only influenced by the movement and changing intensity of weather systems, but also by a ship's movement relative to weather disturbances.

Marine data are invaluable because there are currently so many gaps in weather knowledge concerning the world's oceans. The use of moored and drifting buoys has increased in recent years to provide forecast centres with improved coverage of many areas of the oceans. They house automatic sensors that report, for example, dry bulb and wet bulb temperatures, wind direction and speed, atmospheric pressure and sea-surface temperature.

▲ *An automatic weather buoy* floating in the ocean.

UPPER-AIR

Today, there are 600–650 stations around the world where, twice a day at 0000 and 1200 UTC, balloon-borne instrument packages are released. These radiosondes sense pressure, dry bulb temperature, relative humidity, wind speed and direction as they ascend for about an hour into the lower stratosphere before the helium-filled balloon bursts. The data are transmitted to the release point as the balloon ascends and, in some cases, as the instrument package descends beneath a parachute.

▼ *Distribution of 1200 UTC* upper air reports received on one day at ECMWF (see caption, right), Reading, UK.

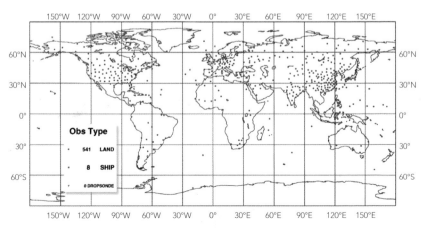

Although the balloon drifts away from its release point, and the readings are taken over the course of an hour or so, meteorologists use the profiles of temperature, etc., as if they were vertical and instantaneous. The temperature and humidity data for an ascent are plotted on special diagrams, either manually or automatically, after which the forecaster can use the profiles as an aid to making a prediction.

Information on the change of wind speed and direction with height is also useful for the forecaster. In addition to the two balloons released at 0000 and 1200 UTC, wind data only are gathered at 0600 and 1800 UTC. One way of measuring the wind during a radiosonde's flight is to use radar to track a 'target' hanging from it.

▲ *Release of a radiosonde* balloon-borne instrument package that relays frequent pressure, temperature and relative humidity observations back to the launch site.

▼ *Distribution of drifting* (red dots) and moored (blue squares) buoys for one day's 12 UTC reports received at the European Centre for Medium-Range Weather Forecasts (ECMWF), Reading, UK.

UPPER AIR OBSERVATIONS AT FOUR STATIONS									
STATION		LERWICK		STAVANGER		LYON		ESSEN	
P (mbar)	H (dm)								
Surface		250	14	325	08	350	01	350	02
925	80	260	23	315	29	205	11	360	02
850	150	260	23	315	33	185	12	060	12
800	210	260	22	310	31	190	11	305	12
700	300	280	24	310	33	200	09	295	23
600	420	285	41	310	43	215	06	295	21
500	540	280	50	310	43	230	11	295	31
400	720	290	64	310	56	250	18	295	49
300	900	305	84	310	62	260	29	290	58
250	1050	320	110	310	58	255	37	290	58
200	1200	310	59	310	56	255	46	295	60
150	1350	300	45	315	51	265	25	300	31

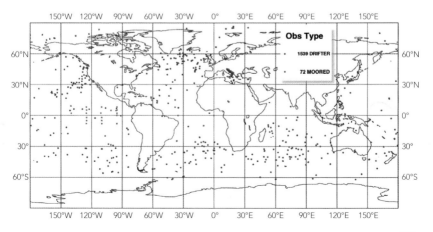

▶ *Canadian precipitation radar sites*. The shaded circle shows the limit of the radar view. The radars emit radiation, small particles of which will be reflected back by precipitation-size particles. This reflected radiation is then translated into an image displaying rainfall rate.

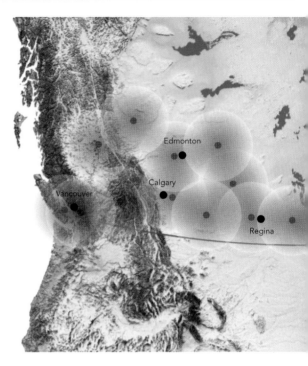

▼ *Spread of radar beam* (2° width) with 1.5° elevation as a function of height and horizontal distance.

All upper-air observations, like surface data, are transmitted to weather forecast centres around the world so that they can be incorporated into computer-based weather prediction models. As with any form of weather data, they must have been checked for quality and have been transmitted as quickly as possible. High-quality and 'fresh' observations are essential for effective weather forecasting.

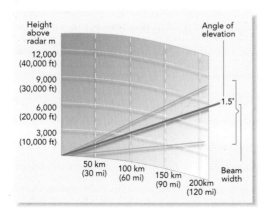

RADAR

Weather services in many developed countries have either complete geographical coverage by precipitation radars, or regional facilities that provide mapping only in heavily populated areas.

Precipitation totals can vary significantly over very short distances, because of this, the spot values recorded by rain gauges (*see pages*

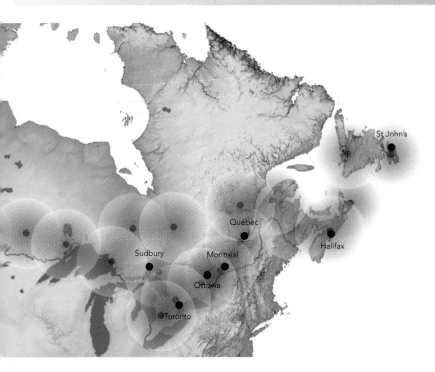

95–96) cannot give a complete picture. The solution lies in the images, or maps, provided by precipitation radars. These make a circular scan at a variety of shallow inclined angles every 15 minutes, or less frequently. They emit pulses of radiation, small fractions of which will be reflected back to the antenna by precipitation-size particles (not by cloud droplets, which are much smaller). The radar converts the reflected radiation into an image showing the rainfall rate. Radars display rainfall out to a radius of some 150 km (90 mi) as a pattern of boxes 1 km (0.6 mi) square, each of which contains an instantaneous average rainfall rate.

▼ *An autographic daily rain gauge strip chart.* Rain gauges measure precipitation levels at the ground, while radar measures the intensity and extent of precipitation on its way down.

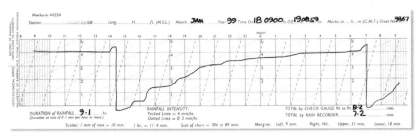

The effectiveness of radar mapping depends on the type of precipitation and its distance from the radar. The nature of the radar itself and the prevailing atmospheric conditions also have an effect.

While gauges register precipitation at the surface, radars can only measure the extent and intensity of precipitation on its way down. This is because a radar's field of view is affected by 'ground clutter' (buildings, hills, etc.). Consequently, the raw data produced by radar must be modified to represent surface values by using a small number of 'check' gauges.

Because the radar beam is emitted at a shallow inclined angle, it views progressively higher elevations the further it is from the radar. This means that it may miss precipitation in some areas.

▲ **The track of an NOAA polar orbiter.**
There are currently two such orbiters. They provide meteorologists with high-quality images of the Earth's surface and clouds.

SATELLITES

Polar orbiters

A significant development for meteorological observation occurred on April 1 1960, when the American TIROS-1 satellite (TIROS stands for Television and Infrared Observational Satellite) was launched from Cape Canaveral, Florida, USA. It entered orbit at an average height of 720 km (450 mi) and provided meteorologists with a new and startlingly view of the Earth in the form of about 23,000 cloud pictures. Its operations were terminated after 78 days when its batteries were exhausted by a transmitter's failure to switch off. Although some US polar orbiters that observe the planet's cloud cover are still named TIROS, most often, these are known as the NOAA satellites, after the National Oceanic and Atmospheric Administration, the US government agency that operates them.

These NOAA satellites are part of a network that forms a crucial component of the global weather observing system today. Currently, there are two such satellites in near-circular orbits, roughly at right angles to each other, at a height of 850 km (530 mi). The height of a satellite determines its

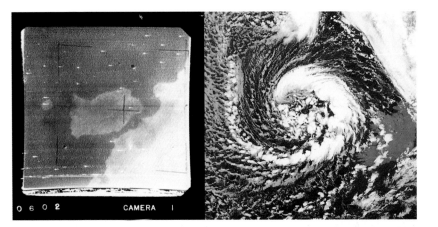

period – the time it takes to circle the Earth once. For a NOAA satellite, this is 102.1 minutes. Today's NOAAs weigh just over 1.7 tonnes and require power of 475 Watts from their solar paddles when all systems are working.

There are other weather polar orbiters, including the Russian Meteor series at a higher elevation of around 1,190 km (740 mi) and a period of 109.4 minutes.

Polar orbiters look down at the planet from a relatively low altitude, around 1,000 km (620 mi), which is only about 0.08 of the Earth's diameter. They provide meteorologists with high-quality images along a swathe of the Earth's surface that shifts from one orbit to the next as the planet rotates beneath the satellite. For the NOAA orbiters, each swathe

▲ *Early and modern satellite images. An early TIROS-I image of Tiburon Island, Gulf of California, 1960 (left) and a thermal infrared image of a showery polar air trough west of Ireland.*

▼ *Field of view of a geosynchronous satellite. They cannot view the highest latitudes.*

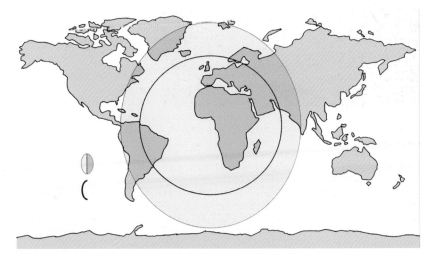

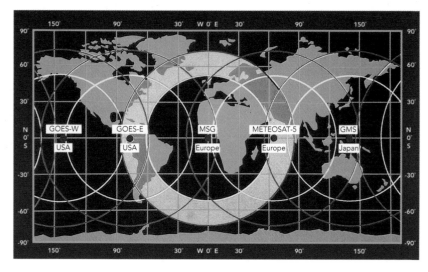

just touches the previous one at the equator, but overlaps progressively more towards the poles. This provides very good temporal coverage at high latitudes, but less frequent imagery within the tropics.

Geosynchronous orbiters

If a satellite is launched to 36,000 km (22,400 mi) above the equator, its complete orbit takes 24 hours. This, of course, is far higher than the NOAA satellites. At 2.8 Earth diameters from the Earth's surface, such a satellite is a long way out in space. This is called the geosynchronous (or geostationary) orbit, because the period of a satellite is the same as the time the Earth takes to rotate once about its axis. Thus, the satellite keeps pace with the spinning planet, racing along eastwards at a speed of just over 3 km/sec (2 mi/sec) and appearing to hover above a fixed point on the equator.

This type of orbit ensures that the satellite always sees the same 'full-disc' face of the Earth, producing a new image of either all or part of the region every 30 minutes. These can be put together to produce an animation for a given period.

There are five weather satellites distributed fairly evenly around the equator, operated by different agencies. Meteosat's are run by the European weather satellite organization, known as EUMETSAT; the two US GOES (Geo- stationary Operational Environmental Satellite) orbiters are overseen by NOAA and GMS (Geostationary Meteorological Satellite) is operated by the Japanese Meteorological Agency.

▲ *The network of geosynchronous weather satellites.*
Each satellite keeps pace with the spinning planet, appearing to hover above the same fixed point. The satellites provide images of their region at 30 minute intervals (15 for Meteosat/MSG) thereby recording any changes in the weather.

Satellite observations

All weather satellites look down at the Earth to produce images of clouds, and many of them reveal the atmosphere's invisible water vapour, too. They do this with an instrument called a radiometer, which is capable of sensing the intensity of radiation coming from the planet. The signal measured is an expression of the strength of, for example, the sunshine reflected back to space by all the surfaces being illuminated.

As the sensor scans the Earth, during daylight hours, it will 'see' very strong reflections, from fresh snow or the tops of very deep clouds. In contrast, it will sense a weak signal from cloud-free vegetated or ocean surfaces that naturally reflect considerably less 'visible' solar radiation. The term 'visible' is used because the waveband employed is more or less that to which our eyes are attuned. Although the images are usually processed in black and white, the scenes are what we would see (in colour) if we were sitting on the satellite!

A full-disc visible image from Meteosat illustrates cloud patterns as various shades of white. The cloud-free areas are darker shades, the tone of which depends partly on the surface viewed and its albedo or reflective strength. Generally, the ocean reflects less than 10% of sunshine falling on it and therefore appears black; the sandy Sahara is quite bright with an albedo of between 25% and 40%. Clean, dry snow reflects something like 75–95%. Clouds reflect more the deeper they are, so thin ones have albedos of 30–50%, while thicker ones are brighter with values between 60% and 90%.

▲ *Meteosat full-disc visible image.* Strong reflectors like clouds appear white while poor ones like the sea appear black.

▼ *Meteosat full-disc thermal infrared image.* Cold surfaces like clouds appear white.

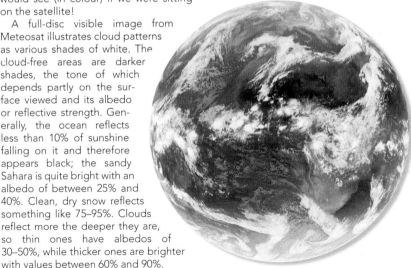

109

One important drawback of visible images is that they are not available during the night. Weather, however, can be raging during the hours of darkness, and meteorologist need to know what is happening to the cloud-laden distur bances around the clock. This is where another common waveband comes into play.

In addition to monitoring short wave 'visible' radiatio that has come from the Sun and is reflected back into space all weather satellites image the planet in the therma infrared, which is a waveband that our eyes do not sense.

The strength of the infrared signal varies with the temper ature of the body that emits it. This will range, for example from an intensely hot, cloud-free Saharan surface (nea 60–70°C [140–158°F]) to the frigidly cold cloud tops of equa torial cumulonimbus thunderclouds at −70°C (−94°F), o sometimes even colder. The hotter a body is, the stronger it signal will be.

Infrared data are mapped and displayed as a black and-white image in such a way that a strong signal appear black, and a weak one white. This way, clouds, whicl are colder than most other surfaces, stand out as white features (see infrared globe, page 106).

One great advantage of the thermal infrared is that it i emitted constantly and, therefore, provides round-the-cloc images. The thermal infrared image that matches the 'visible' image for the same day illustrates the difference between these two wavebands.

Weather satellites also sense additional wavebands including one from which images of water vapour can also be produced. NOAA pola orbiters monitor in five differen channels, while the new serie of Meteosat, called Meteosa Second Generation (MSG) ha started with the operationa 'switch on' of Meteosat 8 or 29 January 2004. This satellite senses the Earth in 12 channels every 15 minutes, at a resolutio suitable for visible (reflected sunlight) images of 1 km (0.6 m directly vertically below the weather satellite.

In addition to their imaging missions, some weather satel lites provide thousands o vertical profiles each day o temperature and humidity down through the atmosphere These are used in compute forecast models, as are the

▼ *False-colour image of cyclone Gafilo* from *Meteosat-8, March 6 2004. The severe Tropical Cyclone Gafilo was one of several cyclones to affect Madagascar in the 2003–2004 season. The image shows cyclone Gafilo about 18 hours before it made landfall. It shows the marked spiral structure of Gafilo and a relatively large eye, with the eyewall and the Central Dense Overcast (CDO) region.*

thousands of cloud-drift winds produced daily by the geosynchronous orbiters. EUMETSAT generates these automatically from sequences of three half-hourly full-disc images centred on 0000, 0600, 1200 and 1800 UTC.

At 1130 UTC, for example, specific cloud types that are known to be reasonably good 'tracers' of the wind are classified automatically on the image. The shapes of these areas are automatically located on the next image 30 minutes later, and on the third image at 1230 UTC. The scheme then estimates the direction and speed of the cloud masses by comparing the first and third images – and allots a value to the middle image time. In this way, a significant number of extra wind observations are made available for regions where there are very few or no radiosondes.

Data relay
Most weather satellites provide a reliable means of communicating weather and other environmental data in real time from remote surface sites. In addition, Meteosat relays observational data, weather analysis and forecast charts around the clock to national meteorological centres in Africa, for example, where they are often not received by the more traditional landline system. Charts are 'uplinked' from the UK's Met. Office in Exeter, while observational data are transmitted from the French and Italian HQs in Toulouse and Rome.

MAPPING THE WEATHER

The surface chart
Synoptic charts, which portray a 'snapshot' of the surface weather across a region, are the working material for many forecasters. They summarize succinctly a vast amount of detail about the weather that can be appreciated very quickly indeed.

The international collaboration that ensures the global transmission of weather observations is extended to the way in which weather maps are plotted. Once received, the various observations are plotted either automatically or by hand on to surface charts. No matter what the scale, however, the manner in which they are represented graphically is dictated by international agreement. Meteorologists represent all of their observations on a map by means of an agreed 'station model', around which all the weather measures are plotted at specific points. Some of the values are coded while others are 'actual'.

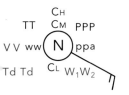

▲ *Plotting convention* *used to indicate a surface station on land.*

Temperature
To the top and left of the station is the dry bulb temperature (TT) plotted to the nearest whole degree Celsius.

Humidity

This is represented by the dewpoint temperature (T_dT_d), plotted at the bottom left. This is the temperature to which the air must cool – at constant pressure and humidity mixing ratio – for it to reach saturation. It is deduced from the dry bulb and wet bulb screen temperatures.

Using hygrometric tables, it is possible to determine the relative humidity for a given dewpoint and dry bulb temperature. The closer the dry bulb and dewpoint, the larger the relative humidity. In addition, for a given pressure, the humidity mixing ratio of the air can be established from its dewpoint temperature.

Pressure

Mean-sea-level pressure (PPP) is plotted to the top and right of the station. It is given to the nearest tenth of a millibar but without the decimal point and the units representing hundreds and thousands. This means, for example, that a pressure of 1,035.7 mbar will be plotted as 357. Similarly, a value of 987.2 is written as 872.

There is never any uncertainty as to whether 357 means 1,035.7 or 935.7 mbar; the analyst always knows which it is from the context of the chart. The main problem caused by these coded values occurs when isobars are being drawn on the maps: the meteorologist must remember that one or two digits are missing. Isobaric analyses are often drawn automatically nowadays.

Immediately to the right of the station is the pressure tendency (ppa), which represents the net change of mean-sea-level pressure during the previous three hours (in mbar and tenths) along with the nature of the change. Thus, 31/ means 3.1 mbar rising, 103\ means 10.3 mbar falling, and 12 ✓ means 1.2 mbar falling then rising more.

Wind direction and speed

If conditions are calm, the wind has no speed and, therefore, no direction. This is noted by a concentric circle around the station circle. Otherwise, the wind direction is represented as a 'shaft' that points towards the centre of the station circle along the direction from which the wind blows. A northerly wind (direction 360 degrees), for example, will be shown by a shaft that runs from due north down to the station, while a south-westerly (from 225 degrees) will be represented by a shaft that points to the centre from the bottom left. Wind direction is reported to the nearest ten degrees and, ideally, plotted with that precision.

▼ **Plotting convention** *for wind observations on a surface chart.*

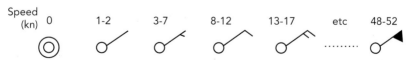

| Speed (kn) | 0 | 1-2 | 3-7 | 8-12 | 13-17 | etc | 48-52 |

The speed of the wind is reported to the nearest knot (roughly 0.5 m/sec [about 2 ft/sec]) and is represented as a 'barb' or barbs at the end of the direction shaft. Wind speeds are rounded to the nearest five knots before plotting. In the northern hemisphere, the speed barbs are drawn on the left side of the shaft, looking towards the station circle; in the southern hemisphere, they are drawn on the right.

Cloud amount

Cloud cover is assessed to the nearest eighth, or 'okta', of the sky. Zero means no cloud at all, while eight eighths indicates total cover or overcast. A small area of blue or a starry patch gives seven eighths and, believe it or not, a recording of nine eighths is also valid. It means that the sky is obscured – by fog or a duststorm, for instance – so the observer cannot report the actual cloud cover.

The total amount of cloud (N) is often made up of overlapping layers and is represented by shading the station circle as shown (left).

Cloud type

The international code for cloud types provides 27 different symbols spread evenly between the three levels.

Once all the types of cloud have been logged, they are plotted such that any low cloud (C_L) is shown below the station circle, any middle cloud (C_M) immediately above it, and any high cloud (C_H) above the middle cloud. On days when there are many different cloud types, the plotted station looks very 'busy'!

Visibility

This is indicated by a two-digit code (VV) to the left of the station circle, outside the present weather symbol if there is one. Since information on poor visibility is of greater use than fine gradations of good or very good visibility, the code is organized so that half of the range of numbers relates to visibility at 5 km (3 mi) or less, as indicated in Chapter 2.

Therefore, plotted values from 01 to 50 represent visibility in tenths of a kilometre: 41 means 4.1 km and 25 indicates 2.5 km. Numbers between 51 and 55 are not used, while from 56 to 80, the increment becomes 1 km after subtracting 50 from the plotted number. Thus, 57 means 7 km and 73 is used for 23 km. The range from 80 to 89 increases in jumps of 5 km such that 80 is 30 km, 81 is 35 km and so on. Finally, the range from 90 to 99 is reserved for visibility observations taken from ships, drilling rigs and some coastal stations where fine resolution is not possible. The poorest visibility would be given as 90, and the best as 99.

Present and past weather

If there is 'weather' when the observation is made, a symbol

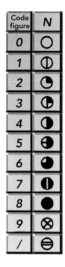

▲ **Plotting convention** *for cloud amount on surface and upper air charts.*

▼ **Symbols for low** *(C_L), middle (C_M) and high (C_H) cloud types.*

	LI	LC	MI	MC	HI	HC
Snow	✳	✳✳	✳✳	✳✳	✳✳✳	✳✳

The abbreviations mean:

LI/LC — light/intermittent/continuous

MI/MC — moderate/intermittent/continuous

HI/HC — heavy/intermittent/continuous

There is a different symbol for showery precipitation to distinguish it from the above. So, for light showers the following pertain:

rain shower   snow shower ⛆   hail shower △

▶ *Plotted surface chart* (*triangular stations are automatic sites*). *Past weather* (W_1W_2) *is plotted to the bottom and right of the station with a choice of ten sorts.*

◀ *Rain, snow and drizzle* *symbols.*

▼ *Weather symbols* *and their definitions (numbers read vertically and then horizontally).*

WW	0	1	2	3	4	5	6	7	8	9
0				∿		S	$/₈	⚡	(⟳)	
1	=	☰	☰	⟨	☋	)•(	(•)	Ҡ	∀	)(
2	⸴]	•]	✳]	✳]	∼]	☋]	✳]	☋]	≡]	Ҡ]
3	↯|	↯	|↯	↯|	↯	|↯	⇸	⇸	⇻	⇻
4	(≡)	☷	≡|	≡|	☰	☰	|☰	|☰	⊻	⊻
5	⸲	⸴⸴	⸵	⸴⸴⸴	⸵⸴	⸴⸵⸴	∼	∼	⸵	⸵
6	•	••	⸵	••	⸵	⸷•	∿	∿	⸵✳	⸵✳
7	✳	✳✳	✳✳	✳✳	✳✳	✳✳	↔	⇢	✳	△
8	⸵▽	⸵▽	⸵▽	⸵▽	⸵▽	✳▽	✳▽	△▽	△▽	△▽
9	⸵▽	Ҡ]•	Ҡ]⸵	Ҡ]✳	Ҡ]✳	•/✳ Ҡ	△ Ҡ	•/✳ Ҡ	↯ Ҡ	△ Ҡ

PRESENT WEATHER

00 to 19	No precipitation at the site at the time of observation.	50 to 59	Drizzle.
		60 to 69	Rain (68 and 69 are sleet).
20 to 29	Precipitation, fog or thunderstorm at the site in the past hour, but not at the time of the observation.	70 to 79	Non-showery solid precipitation.
		80 to 90	Showery precipitation.
30 to 39	Duststorms, sandstorms, drifting or blowing snow.	91 to 94	Precipitation, but with thunderstorm in the past hour.
40 to 49	Fog or ice fog.	95 to 99	Precipitation with thunderstorm.a

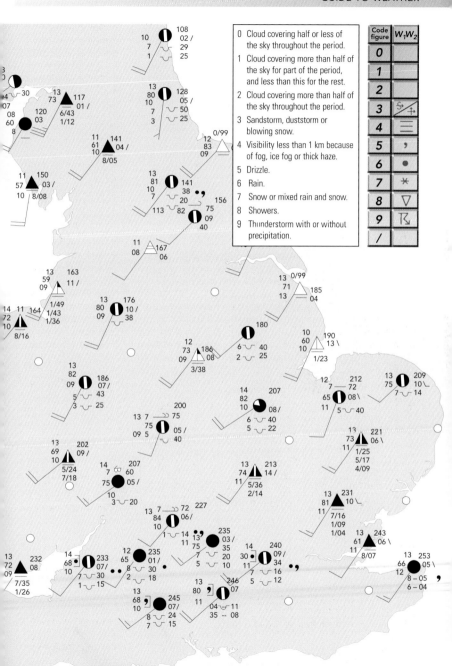

0 Cloud covering half or less of the sky throughout the period.

1 Cloud covering more than half of the sky for part of the period, and less than this for the rest.

2 Cloud covering more than half of the sky throughout the period.

3 Sandstorm, duststorm or blowing snow.

4 Visibility less than 1 km because of fog, ice fog or thick haze.

5 Drizzle.

6 Rain.

7 Snow or mixed rain and snow.

8 Showers.

9 Thunderstorm with or without precipitation.

Code figure	W_1W_2
0	
1	
2	
3	
4	
5	
6	
7	
8	
9	
/	

(ww) is plotted immediately to the left of the station circle. The amount of precipitation is not usually represented on a synoptic chart. However, the occurrence of precipitation – either when the observation was made or since the previous observation – is plotted. In addition, precipitation can be included as an ingredient of the past weather.

Rain, snow or drizzle that falls from extensive sheets of cloud is indicated by the use of symbols that represent both the duration and intensity of the precipitation. These are illustrated in the yellow table at the top of page 114.

The grid on page 114 shows all the symbols used and their broad definitions (table below).

▶ *Typical weather mapping* illustrating basic thermal and wind changes across warm (top left and right) and cold (middle and bottom) fronts.

ANALYSING AND INTERPRETING THE WEATHER MAP

Isobars

Modern weather services provide automatically plotted surface charts, upon which the analyst (or a computer-driven machine) will draw a variety of lines. The main features of interest in middle latitudes are the travelling lows, highs and fronts that produce the varied weather across such regions.

Often the first lines to be drawn are the isobars, which join points of equal mean-sea-level pressure, because this determines the location and intensity (by the central value and surrounding pressure gradients) of the weather-producing

▼ *An example of isobars* plotted onto a weather map. The lines link areas of equal mean-sea-level-pressure. By comparing maps for different times, forecasters can see how the areas of pressure are moving.

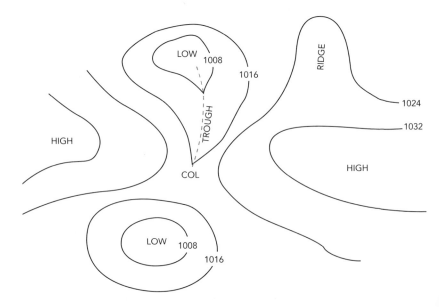

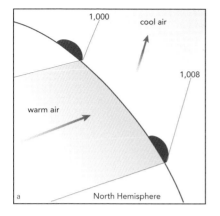

a North Hemisphere

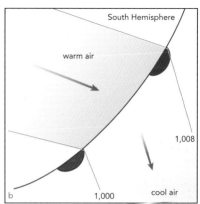

b

disturbances: the lows, the highs, the troughs and the ridges. By comparing successive charts, the forecaster can then determine how they are moving and evolving.

The terms 'low', 'high', 'trough', 'ridge' and even 'col' are evocative of the features shown on topographical maps of the land surface. Indeed, this is why the terms are used; the isobaric map can be thought of loosely as a topographical map, with troughs as 'valleys' and ridges as 'ridges'. An atmospheric col is the equivalent of its topographic namesake, too – a region of weak pressure gradient between two ridges and two troughs. Highs and lows may be many hundreds, or even a few thousand kilometres across.

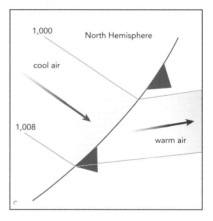

c

Producing an isobaric analysis not only maps these features, but given the strength of the pressure gradient and the alignment of the isobars, also provides valuable information about the surface wind strength and direction. Tightly packed isobars on a chart represent a steep horizontal pressure gradient and thus, very strong winds.

Fronts
Isobars are relatively easy to analyse, whereas much more skill is required to spot fronts (see pages 56–61) on a surface chart. Important weather features in middle and higher latitudes, these are

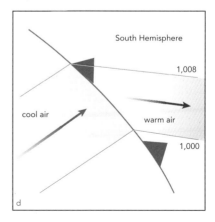

d

shallow, sloping zones that separate extensive air masses that have different values of temperature and humidity, for example.

Cold and warm fronts are the leading edges of cold and warm air masses that sweep generally towards lower or higher latitudes respectively. They are often indicated by a change in the orientation of isobars running across them, in association with a change of wind direction between the air masses that they separate.

UPPER AIR

Weather observations gathered from radiosondes and other platforms, like satellites, are plotted on upper air charts to represent conditions at a variety of levels above the surface. The data plotted on these charts are dry bulb and dewpoint temperature, wind direction and speed, and the height of the pressure surface above mean-sea-level (see the chart

▼ *Typical weather mapping* indicating the height of the 500 mbar surface (dm) above mean-sea-level (solid contours) and the vertical distance between 1,000 and 500 mbar (dm) (dashed contours). Larger values of this 'thickness' indicate a warmer layer, smaller values indicate a colder layer.

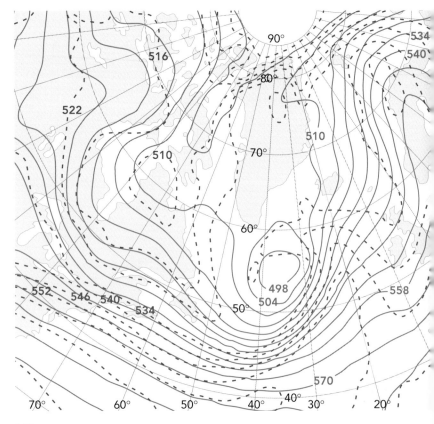

below). The observations can be analyzed in various ways. Tightly packed solid contours on the chart, for example, indicate that very strong, southwest winds were blowing above the central North Atlantic.

It is common for analysts to draw contours of the height of the pressure surface above mean-sea-level at, for example, intervals of 60 m (about 200 ft). This produces a topographical map of the pressure surface which, like a surface weather map, displays ridges, troughs and steep gradients. It is possible to calculate the wind speed from the steepness of the isobaric surface's slope.

Mapping the upper-air features illustrates the presence of the great snaking flow of the wind in the narrow jet-streams, and the slowly-evolving 'long' or 'Rossby' waves that are intimately linked to the intensity and motion of the surface weather.

FORECASTING THE WEATHER

FORECASTING TODAY

The meteorologist who appears in front of millions of viewers is at the sharp end of the forecasting process. What he or she says about the weather represents the culmination of a truly global effort to collect, transmit and process vast amounts of weather data from a variety of widely scattered sources. The television forecaster is backed by a cast of thousands around the globe, whose tasks may include releasing radiosondes in the Antarctic, piloting large commercial aircraft, or serving on coastguard duty. The list of full- and part-time providers of weather data is virtually endless. Not only do national weather services maintain observation sites, but the wide range of professionals whose jobs are affected by the vagaries of the weather are also stalwart providers.

The truly international, free exchange of weather data is a hallmark of the profession of meteorology – and necessarily so. The atmosphere knows no national frontiers; it is only in times of international belligerence that such information is withheld to disadvantage an adversary. So, what you see on television, hear on the radio or read in a newspaper is unique; no other profession provides forecasts with such frequency and under such scrutiny.

How are forecasts made?

The raw ingredients of a weather forecast are the observations taken simultaneously around the world from widely varying platforms. It is a summary of a vast array of constantly updated data. On a typical day, this is the data collated by one of the world's leading weather forecast centres, the European Centre for Medium-Range Weather Forecasts (ECMWF) in Reading, Berkshire, in the UK. The data it collects on a typical day includes:

8,583 SATOBs, estimates of the wind speed and direction gained by tracking the clouds from geo-synchronous satellites like MSG (*see page 108*). Only those cloud types that are known to be reasonably reliable tracers of the air's motion are used. They are monitored within a circle of radius 55 degrees of latitude centred on the sub-satellite point, mainly for upper and lower tropospheric levels;

▼ *Grid points across a sector* of the ECMWF operational global forecast model. The operational forecast model calculates many variables including temperature, wind direction and speed and snow cover at 138,346 grid points on the Earth's surface.

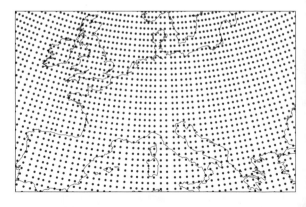

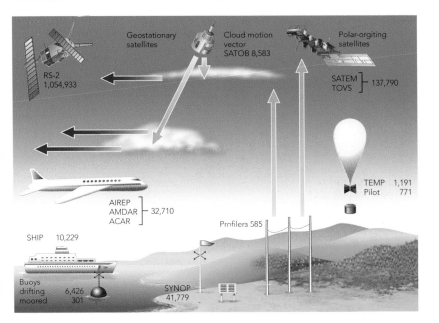

137,790 SATEM and TOVS (TIROS Operational Vertical Sounder) vertical profiles of temperature and humidity, sensed by NOAA polar orbiting satellites. TOVs are received direct from the satellite itself. SATEMs, reduced-resolution versions of TOVs, are transmitted via the WMO's Global Telecommunications System after processing in the USA;

1,054,938 observations from ERS-2 (the European Remote-Sensing Satellite) giving estimates of sea-surface winds. These are deduced from the satellite's measurement of the roughness of the sea's surface using radar;

32,710 AIREP, AMDAR (Automatic Meteorological Data Relay) and ACAR aerial observations from commercial aircraft, either automatically sensed and transmitted, or sent directly from the flight deck by senior staff;

1,191 TEMP reports representing the information from radiosonde ascents made around the world. They include data on temperature, humidity, and wind direction and speed up to a height of about 30 km (19 mi);

771 PILOT observations taken by tracking optically the drift of small balloons to deduce the winds, mainly in the lower troposphere. The data are restricted by the balloon vanishing into cloud or becoming too small to see;

▲ *The various* ***observations used*** *in forecasting the weather. The numbers shown are the total observations received on a typical day at ECMWF, UK. Descriptions of the various methods are detailed on this page.*

585 Profiler observations from automatic instruments that sense wind strength and direction in the lower troposphere. Currently, these are restricted to the USA;

41,779 SYNOP weather reports from the traditional surface weather stations on land, including the growing number of automated sites;

10,229 SHIP surface observations, mainly made from roving commercial vessels;

6,727 observations from moored and drifting buoys, which complete the surface picture across the oceans.

▶ *Levels in the* ***ECMWF*** *operational global forecast model. These are the surfaces on which all the various weather measures have to be calculated at grid points. They are most crowded where the 'action' is - near the Earth's surface and troposphere.*

Computer models

Meteorological computer models apply the unevenly scattered surface and upper-air data to a regular latitude/ longitude grid that has a number of levels up through the atmosphere. At ECMWF, for example, the operational global forecast model grid currently has a horizontal spacing of about 60 km (40 mi). At each of the 138,346 grid points on the Earth's surface, there are values of temperature, wind direction and speed, and humidity, plus soil moisture and snow cover. The Centre's operational model has 31 levels in the vertical, too. These stretch from the surface up to 30 km (20 mi). This means that calculations of the future values of temperature, wind and humidity are currently carried out at 4,154,868 points through the atmosphere.

Some of the raw data cannot be made available when the main observations are taken – from satellites, for example.

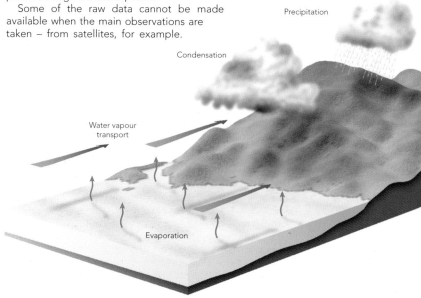

Precipitation

Condensation

Water vapour transport

Evaporation

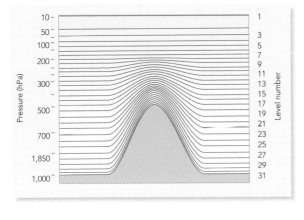

These asynoptic data can be accepted into the computer forecast models when they arrive – as the models are actually running – to produce a prediction.

The computer inserts the values of temperature, humidity, wind and so on into predictive equations that forecast how the situation will change over quite short periods of time, like a few tens of minutes, at every grid point. Many more values are assessed at these points, including the vertical motion of the air's flow. The forecasts for 12, 24, 48 hours, etc., ahead are generated by running the model over these short time steps out to 10 days ahead.

Overall, computer modelling programs are amazingly complex and continue to improve as our knowledge of the workings and interactions between the atmosphere, the hydrosphere, the lithosphere, the biosphere and the cryosphere advances.

Ensemble forecasts

Recent modifications take into consideration advancements in chaos theory. Chaos relates to a small change in the initial conditions of a forecast (those used to drive the weather forecast – that is, the data received from around the world from the 0000 or 1200 UTC observations) that can lead to a dramatically different prediction. The classic example of a butterfly flapping its wings on one side of the globe and creating a storm on the other is a metaphor for the fact that a very small input to the system can lead to a significant larger effect elsewhere.

While it is impossible for operational meteorologists to represent such a small-scale influence, what they can do is run more than one prediction. This is known as the ensemble method, where many forecasts are run, using slightly different initial conditions for each. The marginal differences simulate the existence of 'flapping butterfly wings', albeit on a rather larger scale, in various locations around the world.

At ECMWF, each operational ensemble run currently involves a total of 51 subtly different initial conditions. Of necessity, these forecasts are at a lower resolution than the main operational forecast, using a grid spacing of 120 km (75 mi) instead.

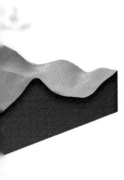

vaporation

▲ *Some of the many processes represented in weather forecast models*

Once the forecasts have been produced, they are grouped into ensembles representing broadly similar predictions. On some days, for example, there may be 30 that point in the same direction, with 12 indicating a different prediction. On another day, the clusters of similar forecasts may be many and consist of only three or four each. In this way, the forecasters can gauge the likely accuracy of the prediction for a certain day. Sometimes, many forecasts indicate the same train of weather events, while on others they are widely different.

▲ *Coarser grid point spacing* *across a sector of the ECMWF global Ensemble Prediction System. The coarser grid allows the system to run a prediction on 51 subtly different weather conditions thus simulating the possible impact of chaos.*

D-I-Y FORECASTS

Noting how cloud formations change over tens of minutes, or a few hours, can lead to an effective forecast for the day ahead.

Showers

Imagine a day when the morning sky starts clear blue, but pretty quickly small scattered cumulus clouds appear. These signify moist bubbles of air that have reached their condensation level. The amount by which they grow up into the troposphere is crucially important in determining the nature of the weather for the day that follows. If the troposphere is unstable – that is, the temperature of the environment through which the cloud is ascending is falling more rapidly than within the cloud – the cumulus cloud will

▼ *Deep cumulus cloud. This type of cloud is usually associated with unsettled weather.*

grow upwards with classic 'boiling' upper reaches. On a good day, it is possible to watch such a cloud for a few minutes and actually observe its top evolving. These 'cauliflower' cumulus clouds are known as cumulus congestus and indicate that the atmosphere is very unstable – where the deep, moist convection penetrates successfully to great heights. If the clouds reach this stage, there is a good chance that a shower will fall from them.

Such shower clouds last for several tens of minutes and produce a swathe of precipitation that may be as wide as the cloud, and perhaps 10 km or more in length. Visibility may be poor in the

▲ **Very deep**, *vigorous cumulonimbus.*

▲ **Scattered shallow cumulus**. *This type of cumulus is known as 'fair weather' cloud.*

▶ **Low level overturning** *below a dry inversion, capped by subsidence. The area above the inversion is usually completely cloud free.*

precipitation, and conditions can be gusty due to the precipitation-induced downdraughts. If convection reaches the top of the troposphere, thunder is likely. An important aspect that determines whether such clouds become the longer-lasting cumulonimbus or shorter-lived, moderately deep cumulus clouds, is wind shear.

If the convective cloud grows in a layer within which the wind does not change much with height, the precipitation that falls back through the cloud's updraught tends to kill it. If, however, there is a marked increase in wind speed with height, the cloud- and precipitation-producing updraught becomes separated from the precipitation-induced downdraught. This separation is a vital ingredient in the longevity of these much deeper convective clouds. Ultimately, they are limited in growth by the stable 'lid' of the tropopause – the zone that caps the troposphere within which temperature remains the same with height (an isothermal layer) or actually increases (an inversion).

If the atmosphere is not so unstable, the shallow clouds will remain as fair-weather cumulus. These will probably grow a little in depth as the surface temperature increases during the day, then slowly decline and die as conditions cool towards evening.

Very often, the vertical extent of these clouds is limited by an inversion within the troposphere, rather than the tropopause itself. The culprit is the subsidence inversion that is found at about 1.0–1.5 km (0.6–0.9 mi) above the surface in anticyclones. The air sinks slowly in great depth

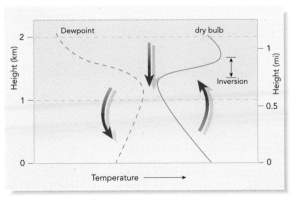

125

to this level, while beneath it, the air is heated from the ground and then churns over to produce cumulus cloud. The subsiding air above the inversion tends to be very dry and completely cloud-free.

This means that although unstable bubbles of moist air ascend through the layer below the inversion, and often experience condensation, the tops of the cloud that forms become flattened at the base of the inversion. In these conditions,

▲ **Very shallow cumulus**, *suppressed by the subsidence above it.*

cumulus clouds adopt pancake-like forms and often spread sideways as continuous sheets of stratocumulus that cover most, or all, of the sky.

Warm fronts

▼ **Pollution across Los Angeles**, *California. High pollution concentrations occur underneath dry inversions.*

▼▶ **Cumulus cloud suppressed** *by subsidence. Sometimes these can spread out to form a continuous sheet of stratocumulus.*

Careful observation of how cloud forms evolve at a particular spot over some hours can also indicate the approach of a warm front. Harbingers of the arrival of a cold front are relatively few. The cloud formations, for example, will be behind the surface front because it tilts backwards, away from the warm sector, trailing its arrival at the surface. Heavy downpours may herald the cold front, as may a veer in the wind direction, although this change is often most noticeable during and immediately after its passage. This is why it is easier for the amateur forecaster to spot an incoming warm front.

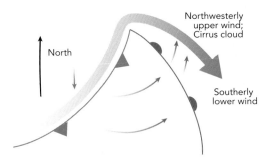

North

Northwesterly
upper wind;
Cirrus cloud

Southerly
lower wind

▲ **Cirrus cloud** usually
approaches from the
northwest (southwest in
southern hemisphere).
Cirrus moves in the
high level cloud flow
ahead of the surface
warm front.

▼ **Cirrus (and contrails)**
can herald the approach
of a distant warm front

▼► **Cirrocumulus cloud**
at sunset.

The warmer, moister air rides up over colder, drier air to form an inclined warm front with a gentle slope of typically 1 in 100, or even more shallow. The upgliding air within the warm sector is marked by condensation that occurs between low levels and the upper troposphere, several hundred kilometres ahead of the front's location on the surface.

Middle-level cloud will occur 200–500 km (120–310 mi) ahead of the surface position, while high cloud will be seen between 500 and 1,000 km (310 and 620 mi) ahead. Therefore, an observer would probably notice the approach of cirrus first of all. A careful watch on this type of cloud usually reveals that it is moving rapidly from the northwest (southwest in the southern hemisphere), around the upper ridge, rather than from the west from which the frontal system itself will likely approach.

If the cirrus is followed over an hour or so by cirrocumulus and/or cirrostratus, this usually indicates the start of a sequence of warm frontal cloud. Cirrostratus has a distinct appearance due to the way in which light from the Sun, or light reflected by the moon, is refracted by the ice crystals from which it is formed. A range of optical phenomena, including 'Sun Dogs' (or Mock Suns) and rings around the Sun or moon, bear witness to the presence of cirrostratus. The former are seen best at times of low Sun, and appear

as two localized bright patches either side of the Sun.

As time passes and the front moves closer to the observer, the cloud will lower, changing to alto-stratus and/or altocumulus cloud at middle levels. The rate at which these changes of cloud type occur will depend on how fast the depression is moving. Often, this will be around 15 m/sec (35 mi/hr), although it can be as much as 25 or 30 m/sec (60 or 70 mi/hr) in vigorous winter storms. If the first cirrus is 1,000 km (620 mi) ahead of a surface front travelling at 15 m/sec (35 mi/hr), it will presage the front's arrival by some 16 or 17 hours.

▲ *Cirrostratus* above *sand dunes.*

▲ *Mock Sun*, or 'Sun Dog' in *cirrostratus.*

Although there may be precipitation from the altostratus, it will not reach the surface. Altostratus cloud may make the Sun look opaque – it appears 'as if through ground glass'.

▼ *Altocumulus* appears at middle levels.

The altiform cloud will be followed by thickening, lowering cloud such as nimbostratus from which the first major precipitation may fall. There-fore, the first rain or snow reaches the ground a few hundred kilometres (about 150 miles) ahead of the surface front and typically lasts for a few to several hours.

The lowest cloud in the sequence occurs close to the surface front, and after this has passed, the sky tends to be laden with stratiform cloud. This can be very extensive or quite broken, especially over, and in the lee of, hilly areas.

In contrast to the general south-eastward movement of cloud at the highest levels ahead of the front, the surface flow will usually be *from* the south-east. The wind will often veer to southwesterly as the front passes.

Various types of cirriform cloud will often be seen in the sky, but they do

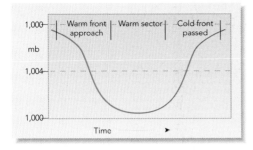

▲ **Barometric pressure change** associated with a frontal system's passage over an observer

▶ **Surface chart depiction** of the approach of a frontal system towards an observer.

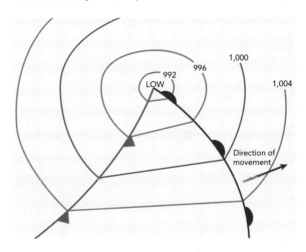

◀ **Atostratus with scud below**. Scud clouds are often formed by condensation due to cooling of the air by evaporating raindrops falling from the higher sheet of cloud.

not necessarily always signify the approach of a front.

The key to a successful amateur weather forecast is being able to recognize the *sequence* of cloud formation. Other good indicators are wind direction, temperature and pressure The approach of a frontal depression leads to a fall in atmospheric pressure. However, this can be complicated by the pressure falling, rising or remaining the same in different regions of the system as it moves across the Earth's surface.

Generally, though, the progress of a warm front towards a spot is linked to a falling barometer. As the front passes, there is usually a weakening or levelling off of the pressure fall, followed by a rise in pressure as the cold front sweeps

through. A fall in pressure usually foretells the imminent arrival of a depression or trough, while a rise is the expression of the gradual improvement of conditions associated with a high or ridge.

The region between warm and cold fronts is often marked by extensive low-layer cloud – especially on windward coasts – and occasional precipitation that is usually heavy shortly before the arrival of the cold front. Conditions are mild and damp in winter, and cool and damp in summer.

Sometimes, the extensive stratiform cloud breaks up inland, especially if over hilly areas. This means that sunny spells can develop, producing much higher temperatures.

ENVIRONMENTAL ISSUES

During the last decade or so, we have become more aware of global, or near-global, changes in the atmosphere that have occurred due to the activities of human society.

Global warming has occurred in the past, even before the existence of the human race; the climate naturally fluctuated over time. However, scientists are certain that the increase of "greenhouse gases" such as carbon dioxide (CO_2) in the atmosphere will lead to a significant rise in surface air temperature in the coming decades. This increase in gas concentration is almost certainly due to the large-scale industrial and agricultural activities of human society – for example factory emissions and the clearing of large sections of the world's rainforests.

Antarctic stratospheric ozone depletion – the so-called 'hole' in the ozone layer – is another environmental problem caused by human activity. The discovery, some two decades ago, of the plunge in ozone concentrations during the southern-hemisphere spring, stimulated rapid and effective international action to ban the gases that scientists had shown to be the culprits.

Industrial society has also managed to generate other types of important atmospheric problems. Like global warming and ozone depletion in the stratosphere, the fluidity of the atmosphere means that impacts can spread a long way from sources of, for example, industrial pollution. Acid rain is a case in point. Additionally, on a more local scale, low-level ozone creation can occasionally be a serious health concern in susceptible areas (*see* page 145).

▼ *Haze and clouds* obscure the setting sun over Antarctica. The Antarctic Peninsula, which amounts to 4% of the continent, is currently warming at a rate of two to three times the global average.

GLOBAL WARMING

Greenhouse gases have been an integral part of the atmosphere for many millions of years. This means that greenhouse gases act as crucially important insulators for the Earth and all life upon it – without them, we would not be here.

There are a number of greenhouse gases, they include carbon dioxide, methane, nitrous oxide and CFCs (their function as greenhouse gases is unconnected with their role in ozone depletion). The significance of these gases lies in their ability to absorb outgoing terrestrial long-wave radiation and re-radiate in all directions, including back down to the surface.

As the Sun's rays pass through the atmosphere on their way down to Earth, some heat is absorbed, but much of the solar energy passes through and is absorbed by the Earth. This energy is reradiated by the Earth as long-wave (infrared, or heat) radiation, which cannot pass easily through the greenhouse gases in the atmosphere and is partially absorbed. Part of this absorbed heat is reradiated to space, but some is reradiated back down to Earth. The gases thus act rather like the glass in a greenhouse and trap heat.

Water vapour is also a powerful greenhouse gas, but at present its total global concentration is not changing significantly. If the surface warms as predicted, however, it would be expected to rise because of increased evaporation from the oceans.

Sources of greenhouse gases

Industrialized society has been increasing the atmospheric concentration of these significant gases for the past century or more. We know from careful monitoring and estimation that carbon dioxide levels in the atmosphere have increased in the last 200 years, from around 200 parts per million (ppm) to about 360 ppm in the late 1990s. We also know that this increase in the atmospheric concentration can be accounted for from international inventories that list the mass of fossil

▼ *Global warming*. *The first diagram shows how the heat is transferred from the Earth surface into space. The greenhouse effect, shown in diagram two, causes gases to absorb part of the outgoing heat and then re-radiate part of it back down to Earth.*

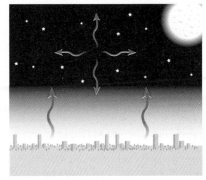

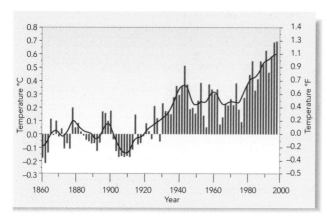

◄ *The rise in air temperature*. This graph depicts the departure of annual global air temperature over land and sea, relative to that at the end of the 19th century.

fuel that is burned every year, along with other contributors of added CO_2. In fact not all the gas that is liberated stays in the atmosphere; a good deal is absorbed by the oceans and, of course, by vegetation. Additionally, the concentration of atmospheric methane has doubled during the last century, while nitrous oxide is increasing at about 0.25% a year. The increase is partly related to rice farming in paddy fields and to the by-product of cattle digestion! These three gases are increasing largely as a result of energy generation, transport and agriculture.

Undoubtedly, human society is changing the composition of the atmosphere. Due to the increase in these and other greenhouse gases, such as the halocarbons CFC-11 and HCFC-22, we can expect to see the impact of an enhanced greenhouse effect. While an international ban has been imposed on such greenhouse gases, their residence time in the atmosphere has long-lasting consequences.

Temperature change

So what has happened to the global average surface temperature over the last century or so? The combined air temperature over land and sea-surface temperature for each year from 1861 to 1997, when compared to the average for the period 1961–90, is illustrated above. Each line above or below the 0.0 axis represents a positive or negative departure in respect of the recent 30-year period. The red curve is a running mean that smoothes out short-term fluctuations.

When averaged around the globe, it would seem that there has been an increase of 0.6°C (33°F) from start to finish during this period. It is important to stress that, although the carbon dioxide has increased markedly during this time, global mean temperature has not risen continuously. There were periods, during the 1940s and 1950s, for example, when it remained constant or even decreased.

Modelling the change

Climate modellers use sophisticated computer simulations to represent the complex physical interactions we know to be important in determining climate and its changes. The variables and the interactions that concern such groups are highlighted below.

The artificial increase in greenhouse gases is only part of the story. The amount of carbon dioxide, for example, that remains in the atmosphere depends on poorly understood aspects of the global carbon cycle. The oceans absorb and release it in certain areas, while the world's vegetation cover also plays an important role, since it is absorbed by plants in the process of photosynthesis.

The study of global budgets of methane, carbon, nitrogen and other substances is still very much in its infancy. However, major international scientific projects have been developed to improve the observational networks, to stimulate research and, ultimately, to deepen our understanding of the reservoirs and the exchanges between them.

The impact of aerosols – very small particles suspended in the atmosphere – must also be considered by climate modellers. Recent work has highlighted the important role played by sulphate aerosols, which emanate from sulphur dioxide emissions and from the evaporation of seawater. They are known to offset the warming effect of greenhouse gases by causing the atmosphere to reflect more solar radiation into space than otherwise would be the case.

▼ *Climate system components* and *interactions. Climate models create examples of environmental scenarios and generate the possible outcomes.*

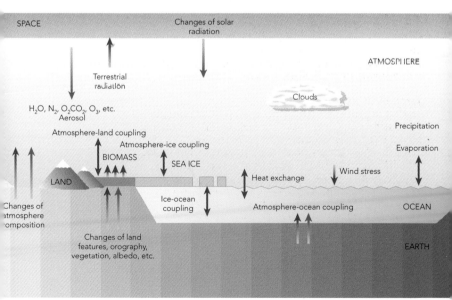

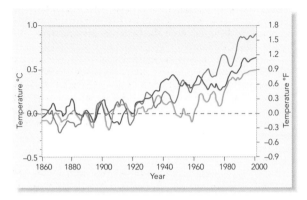

◀ **Observed (red) and simulated** global temperature, including greenhouse gases (blue) plus sulphate aerosols (green). The greenhouse gas simulation in particular produces a steep climb in temperature.

The UK's Hadley Centre for Climate Prediction and Research, which is part of the Met Office, is renowned for its research into climate modelling and has produced a model that seems to capture the essence of global warming. Internationally based climate prediction centres such as those in the USA and Canada have also produced similar results.

Depicted above are the observed global temperature changes since 1860 in red; the computer simulation of change based only on increasing greenhouse gases in blue; and another simulation to which has been added the impact of sulphate aerosols in green. Of course, it would be miraculous to see a perfect, or even near perfect, fit. That said, the simulations have, in essence, followed the fluctuations around the zero line from 1860 to about 1920 and, in the main, have tracked the broad increase since then. For the last 40 years or so of the series, the added-sulphate model has performed best, falling within 0.1°C (0.2°F) of the upward march of global temperature. This does not necessarily mean that the scientists understand the processes well enough to reproduce the observed change in this way, but it is unlikely that the reasonable match occurred by chance.

When the Hadley Centre climate model is run forward in time, assuming an annual increase in atmospheric carbon dioxide of 1 ppm a year, it predicts a mean global warming of 0.3°C (0.5°F) a decade, the most intense increase occurring in the winter across the northern high latitudes. The blue line on the graph opposite illustrates this progression, while the green line simulates the predicted change if sulphates are added – the increase then drops to about 0.2°C (0.4°F) a decade. An important difference in these two constituents is that aerosols remain in the atmosphere for a few days, while carbon dioxide lingers in the atmosphere for something like a century.

If legislation reduced or levelled sulphur dioxide emissions, the model suggests that the full effect of warming due to carbon dioxide increase would soon become apparent. This is illustrated by the purple line.

The models are also used to predict the increase in global mean-sea-level that is expected to occur during the 21st century as the oceans warm and expand. The best estimate, due to this effect, is that the global average increase between now and the end of this century will be 0.25–0.35 m (10 to 13 in). This is a very significant increase and would have dramatic consequences.

Uncertainties

The climate modellers themselves are the first to admit to the imperfections of their simulations, including the representation of clouds. Additionally, not enough is known about the sensitivity of climate to changes in aerosols, volcanic activity and solar output.

A number of groups are currently actively researching in this field and all the models point in the same direction, with varying degrees of intensity and patterns of change. If the release of greenhouse gases into the atmosphere continues at a steady rate, it is estimated that carbon dioxide levels will double from pre-industrial values by the end of the 21st century. Adding the effect of an increase in water vapour and other factors leads to a spread of predictions about the magnitude of the warming by that time. They range from 1.5°C to 4.5°C (2.7°F to 8.1°F), the best estimate lying somewhere around 2.5°C (4.5°F) as a global average.

Nonetheless, there are significant uncertainties in all this work. Some meteorologists refute the idea that an increase in atmospheric water vapour content will lead to a rise in greenhouse warming; they maintain that the increase will

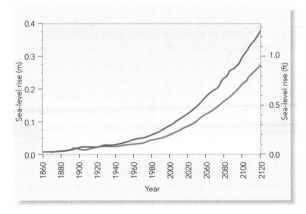

► **Global mean-sea-level increase** due to expansion related only to greenhouse gas increase (blue) plus aerosol increase (green). An increase in both greenhouses gases and aerosols has a dramatic effect on global sea-level.

lead to changes in clouds, such that they will become more efficient at producing precipitation and will therefore rain out a lot of the water that would enhance the greenhouse effect. The real impact of increased water vapour will only become apparent years into the future, when more modelling studies have been undertaken and more observational evidence is available.

At the moment however, it is apparent that an increase in water vapour could very likely lead to an increase in the incidence of cloud and, therefore, a decrease in the amount of solar radiation reaching the surface. This, of course, would be a negative feedback.

Overall, though, even though there are serious sceptics in the scientific community, and the models used to predict future atmospheric conditions are imperfect, a significant majority of atmospheric scientists place faith in the results provided by their peers in this particular field.

Decision time

Governments are listening closely to the predictions and are acting both individually and collectively to reduce the worst impacts of the predicted changes. There have been a number of very high-profile intergovernmental meetings to formulate agreements designed to cut back the output of greenhouse gases. At the 1992 Earth Summit in Rio de Janeiro, Brazil, it was agreed that by 2000, the emissions of carbon dioxide would be stabilized at 1990 levels to slow the rate of increase. To prevent further rises in its atmospheric concentration, a global 60% cut would be required. The likelihood of this happening was remote, to say the least.

By June 1993 a total of 166 nations had signed up to the 'Framework Convention on Climate Change'. This set out the way in which the problem of reducing greenhouse gas emissions could be tackled by concerted international effort. The targets were changed so that, relative to 1990 emission levels, the European Union as a whole must reduce emissions by 8% averaged over the period from 2008 to 2012. The USA's reduction target was set at 7% for the same period. However, the Kyoto Protocol of December 1997 that laid down these principles will not come into force until at least 55 nations ratify it and the accumulated emissions from such nations must not reach less than 55% of the global total. By early July 2004, some 160 countries had ratified it but their emissions totalled 44.2% of world output. The convention had not at that time been ratified by, for example, Australia, Indonesia, the Russian Federation and the USA. Without the backing of international law, however, it is impossible to predict when the protocol will come into force.

OZONE DEPLETION

What is ozone?

For millions of years, the gas called ozone has existed naturally in the Earth's atmosphere and has helped to safeguard life as it has evolved on the planet.

Oxygen is most frequently found in its diatomic form, O_2, in the atmosphere, where it makes up slightly less than 21% by volume. It is the second most common gas in the atmosphere after nitrogen (N_2) and is essential for the maintenance of life on our planet. Ozone, however, is the triatomic form of oxygen O_3 that is produced in the middle to lower stratosphere by the bonding of a single atom (O) and O_2.

Natural creation and destruction

The solar radiation that arrives at the Earth's surface has been changed substantially on its way down through the atmosphere. Some of it is reflected back out to space by clouds, dust layers, and the land and ocean: reflected sunshine is completely lost to the Earth's atmospheric system. On the other hand, some of it is absorbed by the clouds and dust, and, of course, by the surface of the Earth. This absorption heats the substance involved – for example the oceans, icebergs, or land surface.

Most of the solar radiation with wavelengths of up to 0.21 micrometers is absorbed above 50 km (30 mi) by nitrogen and oxygen. The absorption of the solar radiation warms the atmosphere within the ozone layer and also prevents this radiation, which is harmful to life, from reaching the Earth's surface or the lower atmosphere.

Absorption of incoming solar radiation in the range 0.21–0.31 micrometers is carried out principally by ozone within the stratosphere.

Very short-wave ultraviolet radiation, at wavelengths of less than 0.24 micrometers, actually divides an O_2 molecule into two oxygen atoms (O + O). In a split second, these extremely reactive oxygen atoms will combine with other O_2 molecules to produce ozone.

Additionally, ozone is destroyed by being split into O_2 and O by ultraviolet radiation with a wavelength longer than 0.29 micrometers. This process is known as photodissociation. As this demonstrates, stratospheric ozone is not only created naturally, but also destroyed by entirely natural processes.

Creation and destruction are continuous during sunlit hours and, until the

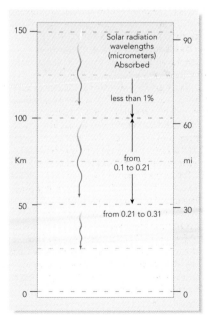

▼ *The absorption of short wave* solar radiation in the high atmosphere. Ozone is created in the lower 50 km (30 mi) of the high atmosphere.

recent problems associated with serious artificial depletion, occurred at about the same rate. This meant that the total amount of the gas remained broadly constant. That said, the balance can be tipped in one direction or the other by the seasonal cycle, by volcanic eruptions, by changes in the intensity of the Sun's output, and by the quasi-biennial oscillation, which is a switch in the flow within the equatorial stratosphere from easterly to westerly and back to easterly over a period of about 26 months.

The heating of the air, caused by the reaction between solar radiation and ozone, is important, because it plays a part in determining the circulation of the atmosphere at high elevations and, to some extent, of the troposphere below. The reason for this is that pressure patterns are strongly influenced by thermal patterns; in their turn, wind direction and strength are determined by the horizontal pattern of pressure.

Where is ozone found?
Not surprisingly, stratospheric ozone is formed mainly within tropical latitudes, where solar radiation is strong throughout the year. However, this is not where the highest concentrations are to be found, as atmospheric circulation transports the ozone to extratropical latitudes.

Ozone values in the tropics are low not only because it is carried away from the region, but also because the stratosphere is shallower there than across higher latitudes. This is because the low-latitude troposphere is typically 18 km (11 mi) deep, whereas it is about a third of that value in the highest latitudes.

The largest amounts of ozone occur in middle latitudes, above Hudson's Bay and eastern Siberia in the northern hemisphere, and around the flank of the Antarctic continent in the southern hemisphere. Concentrations decline towards polar regions, especially over Antarctica.

Even where the highest concentrations are found, in the stratosphere between 12 and 35 km (7 and 22 mi), it represents only about two parts per million by weight. Therefore, it is a gas with a significance far exceeding its minute presence. Until only a couple of decades ago, there was no suspicion that there was any risk at all to this natural shield.

Threats to the ozone layer
In the early 1970s, the thrust, on both sides of the North Atlantic, to construct and fly supersonic transport (SST) passenger aircraft caused some stratospheric specialists to voice concern. To achieve speeds of Mach 2, these aircraft were required to cruise in the lower stratosphere – the region where ozone is most highly concentrated. Scientists were concerned that reactive nitrogen in the SST exhausts might speed up the natural decay of ozone and lead to

significant depletion. As it turned out, only a small number of Concorde SSTs were constructed, the first making its maiden commercial flight to the Gulf in 1976, before being decommissioned in 2003. Since then, the comparative impact of these few aircraft has been insignificant.

Around the time that suspicions about SSTs surfaced, scientists also became concerned about the potential threat to the ozone layer from artificial compounds known as chlorofluorocarbons (CFCs), developed in the 1920s from chlorine, fluorine and carbon. With an extremely stable molecular arrangement, they are non-toxic, non-corrosive, non-flammable and do not react with almost any other substance. These properties led to their use as coolants in refrigerators and air conditioners, as trappers of heat in insulated cups and houses, as spray-can propellants, and as cleaners of delicate electronic components.

▼ *The process of ozone depletion* *due to the release of CFCs into the air. CFCs drift slowly into the stratosphere and are broken down by the Sun's ultraviolet radiation into chemicals that destroy the ozone layer.*

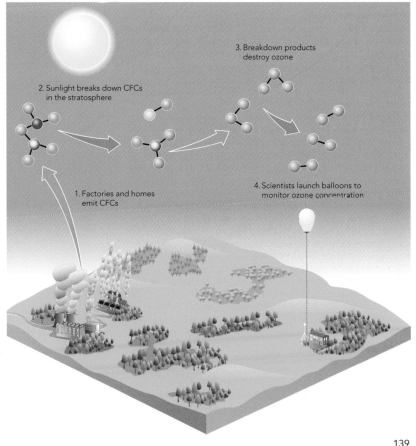

3. Breakdown products destroy ozone

2. Sunlight breaks down CFCs in the stratosphere

1. Factories and homes emit CFCs

4. Scientists launch balloons to monitor ozone concentration

Once released into the air, however, the extreme stability of CFCs meant that they would drift around for years – not only near the surface, but also up in the stratosphere. At these higher altitudes, the very short-wave solar radiation would be able to split their bond to add millions of tonnes of extra chlorine to the stratosphere (this gas does occur there naturally, albeit in very small concentrations, from dimethyl chloride supplied by the oceans).

In the same way that governments face tough decisions today about global warming, political leaders in the early 1970s had to decide whether the scientists' prediction would become a reality. If they believed the experts, massive changes would have to be implemented to slash CFC production and to find safe replacements. Dismissing the scientific assessment would be courting potential disaster on a global scale.

So it was that in 1974 atmospheric scientists set out to learn as much as possible about the complexities of stratospheric chemistry, and about ozone in particular. One problem they encountered was the lack of observations of important chemicals in the stratosphere. Over the following few years, chemists experimented in laboratories to determine the rate at which chlorine could destroy ozone. Others launched special balloons carrying instrument packages to measure the concentrations of key chemicals that help control ozone levels.

By 1976, observations and computer simulations pointed to a serious depletion of stratospheric ozone due to the release of CFCs. The public called for governmental action, but it was not until 1979 that some, including that of the largest producer and user – the United States – stopped the sale of aerosol cans using CFCs as propellants. This led to a quick levelling off of CFC production because spray-cans were the largest consumer of these gases.

The problem persisted, however, because industry still used CFCs in other ways, and by 1985 production of CFCs was increasing at a rate of 3% annually. This significant change stimulated many governments to sign the Vienna Convention for the Protection of the Ozone Layer, which required the parties involved to formulate a plan for global action to curb CFCs. Research accelerated into ozone depletion due to CFCs and also halons, which are related bromine-based compound; use of the latter had increased dramatically during the previous decade because of their efficiency in extinguishing fires.

In the mid-1980s, the best estimate of the reduction in stratospheric ozone pointed to a decrease of some 5% by 2050, which could mean millions of new cases of skin cancer worldwide. This was serious and was compounded by the fact that the halocarbons already injected into the air would remain there for more than a century.

Discovery of the 'hole'

In May 1985, news spread that scientists had discovered massive ozone depletion over parts of the Antarctic during the austral spring. According to news reports, the reduction was so great that there were almost holes in the ozone layer, and the concept stuck.

In fact, there is no region of the stratosphere where there is no ozone, and the discovery in the mid-1980s pointed to severe depletion above the Antarctic alone. There was no question that the depletion in the early spring was real – but was it really due to human society polluting the stratosphere or, perhaps some natural variation?

Massive effort was put into unravelling the problem. In September 1986, a team of scientists travelled to McMurdo Station in the Antarctic to undertake an intensive programme of ground-based and balloon-borne observations. They quickly confirmed the presence of high levels of artificially made, ozone-destroying chemicals.

▼ *The impact of stratospheric ozone* depletion on increased UV at the Earth's surface. The main health effects from exposure to increased UV-B due to ozone depletion include skin cancer, cataracts and accelerated aging of the skin.

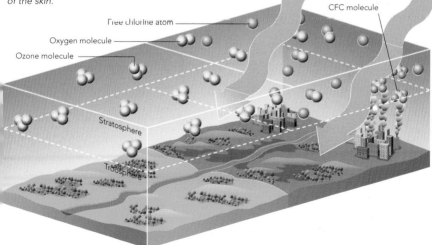

CFC molecule

Free chlorine atom

Oxygen molecule

Ozone molecule

Stratosphere

Troposphere

One year later, in the subsequent austral spring, more than 100 scientists made their way to Punta Arenas in southern Chile. Other scientists returned to McMurdo to repeat their investigations. High-flying U-2 aircraft, carrying special instruments, flew through the intensely cold layers of the lower stratosphere, where depletion was known to occur. The experiment confirmed that chlorine and bromine pollution had indeed led to ozone depletion. The scientific suspicions of a decade before had been confirmed.

▼ The average total ozone for October (1954–94), Halley Bay, Antarctica

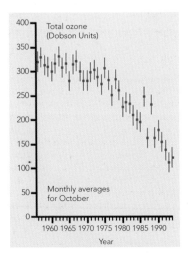

Antarctic depletion explained

The north and south polar regions are distinctly different, being almost total mirror images of each other, in that the Arctic is an ocean surrounded by continents, while the Antarctic is a continent surrounded by the circumpolar ocean. This fact plays a crucial role in the difference between their respective high-level (and low-level) atmospheric circulations.

In the depths of winter, the stratospheric circulation above the Antarctic is a more or less smooth, westerly flow centred near the pole. It is not particularly wavy since it is above the broadly symmetric Antarctic continent. This flow means that very frigid air

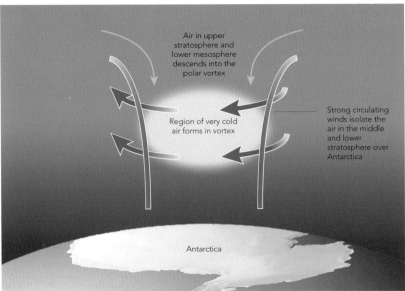

Air in upper stratosphere and lower mesosphere descends into the polar vortex

Region of very cold air forms in vortex

Strong circulating winds isolate the air in the middle and lower stratosphere over Antarctica

Antarctica

▶ **Mean ozone totals** for southern hemisphere, October (1980–91). The purple areas indicate the lowest levels of ozone. Due to the effects of the polar vortex, the ozone hole is greatest over Antarctica leading up to the austral spring.

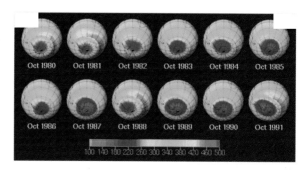

resides inside this spinning well during the southern winter – often plummeting below –80°C (–112°F) – which leads to the formation of polar stratospheric clouds (PSC). Breakdown of ozone occurs when the gas interacts with the CFCs on the ice crystals forming these clouds. When springtime solar radiation starts to increase during September and October, the circulation breaks down, becoming wavy and letting in ozone-rich air from higher latitudes. This raises the concentration of gases to safer levels until the circulation cuts off again as the next winter approaches.

The Arctic is quite different: it is much more susceptible to the incursion of frontal disturbances deep into its interior, particularly through the Norwegian Sea. This means that, in most years, the stratosphere above it does not become cold enough for the formation of PSC and, therefore, does not suffer a similar annual depletion. On occasion, however, some unusually cold winters have led to ozone depletion within the Arctic stratosphere.

The Montreal Protocol

The discovery of serious depletion over the Antarctic spurred governments into action. In September 1987, a meeting of environment ministers from 24 industrialized nations was convened in Montreal, Canada. They agreed a plan of action to reduce CFCs so that the 1986 concentrations would be reduced by 20% by the end of 1994, and by 50% by the end of 1999. This binding agreement, embodied in the Montreal Protocol, represented a new step in intergovernmental collaboration on tackling environmental problems. It was also decided to reconvene in London, in 1990, to establish whether any modifications were needed.

◀ **The Antarctic polar vortex**. The increase in solar radiation in the Antarctic spring causes the wind circulation to break down, letting in ozone-rich air from higher latitudes.

The dramatic springtime ozone depletion persisted – and not only for the austral pole. The Arctic polar region was under intense study in the late 1980s. Depletion occurred there too, but not with the same intensity.

The June 1990 meeting in London declared a complete end to the production of CFCs by 2000, of halons (except for absolutely essential use) by 2000, and of carbon tetrachloride

143

◀ *Stratospheric ozone levels* for Sept 10, 2000 (top) and Sept 11, 2003 (bottom). The size of the 2003 Antarctic ozone hole reached 10.9 million mi² on Sept 11, 2003, slightly smaller than North America, but smaller than the largest ever recorded, on Sept 10, 2000, when it covered 11.5 million mi².

(by 2000) and methyl chloroform (by 2005). Included in this London Amendment were provisions for easier CFC phase-outs by developing countries, and the establishment of a fund to help those countries switch to ozone-friendly replacements.

A further meeting in Copen-hagen, Denmark, in 1992 brought deadlines forward. Thus, all CFC, carbon tetrachloride and methyl chloroform production was to cease by the end of 1995, and halon manufacture even earlier, by the end of 1993. Other harmful agents were to be phased out completely by the end of 2029.

Recent Times

Atmospheric scientists have predicted that the Antarctic (and more general) stratospheric ozone concentrations will probably recover to their pre-artificial depletion levels by around 2050. This estimate is based on complex atmospheric dynamical/chemical models, given the known injection of the troublesome gases and their longevity. Although the Antarctic ozone hole shrank in the southern spring of 2001, it has recently attained its two largest ever extents in the austral springs of 2000 (30 million km² [12 mi²]) and 2003 (26 million km² [10 mi²]).

STREET LEVEL OZONE

In contrast to the serious reduction of the ozone a few tens of kilometres up in the atmosphere, much closer to home is the modern-day increase in its concentration at street level. It may seen paradoxical, but the very same type of gas that protects life on Earth by its presence in the stratosphere can actually threaten life if it occurs even in very small concentration at the Earth's surface. Surface ozone was measured reliably in the 1870s and found to occur at about 10 parts per billion (ppb) in the atmosphere. In the modern industrial world, we know that its concentration can be dangerously increased by sunlight acting upon nitrous oxides and volatile organic compounds in the air. The sun shining on these artificial constituents over a number of hours can create a very unhealthy atmosphere.

The pollutants are released through, for example, the combustion of diesel and other fuel. This indicates that ozone is likely to reach the highest values in large urban areas during the summer when days can be hot and winds light (with not much vertical mixing in anticyclonic conditions). Los Angeles is a prime example of a traffic-choked city with appropriate summertime weather conditions. Other more

▼ *Launching an ozonesonde* from the South Pole station. This balloon transported instrument measures a vertical profile of the ozone layer.

southern US cities like Houston suffer too, as does Athens in Greece. Why is it a problem? If ozone protects us, how can it be a problem? The fact is, as mentioned earlier, Nature's sunscreen is a safe distance above the surface. The reality is that ozone, even in very low concentration, can produce serious and irreversible damage to animal tissue and especially to humans' lungs. Indeed, the World Health Organization (WHO) has issued guidelines for an upper limit of ozone that is considered safe for human exposure – it's 60 ppb of air, averaged over 8 hours. Such a level should not be exceeded on more than 20 days per year too. Such levels have already been exceeded in major Australian cities on occasion and, as an indicator of the extreme nature of Los Angeles' potential problem, an initial smog alert is issued if the con-

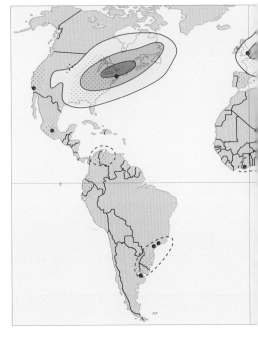

centration exceeds 500 ppb, followed by second and third level alerts if 1,000 then 1,500 ppb are passed. It should be said that this problem is not unique to major US or Australian cities. Unhealthily high ozone concentrations can occur on hot, calm days in not very large, traffic-busy towns across middle latitudes. It is a fact also that the problem gas doesn't stay put in urban areas and can drift, even on light winds, into rural regions.

ACID RAIN

Precipitation is naturally weakly acid. However, in modern times the acidity has been enhanced because of the injection into the atmosphere of artificially-produced sulphur dioxide and nitrous oxides. The former comes from coal-fired power stations and natural gas processing for example, while the latter is produced partly by vehicle emissions and industrial furnaces. Once these gases are emitted, they are transported on the wind and can ultimately combine with atmospheric water to produce weak sulphuric and nitric acid that falls out in the form of raindrops. It is therefore quite likely that the rain (or snow or fog) will fall or develop some hundreds or thousands of kilometres from the gaseous source. Acid rain has the worst impact if it falls on land where there is no

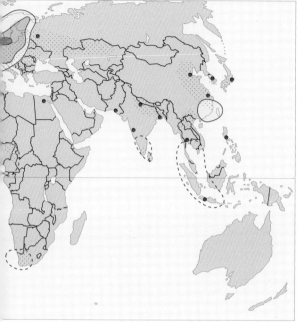

◀ **Regions with high concentrations of acid rain**. *Those places with high levels of acidity (low Ph levels) – are often located away from the dotted areas – those regions with high emission levels. This is because pollution is dispersed by the wind.*

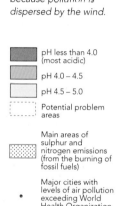

pH less than 4.0 (most acidic)

pH 4.0 – 4.5

pH 4.5 – 5.0

Potential problem areas

Main areas of sulphur and nitrogen emissions (from the burning of fossil fuels)

• Major cities with levels of air pollution exceeding World Health Organization guidelines

natural way of neutralising the acidity. The area of eastern Canada for example has a geology and soil type that means its lakes and vegetation suffer badly as a result of pollution that has come from 'upstream' – normally further west in Canada or from across the border with the USA. Indeed, under certain circumstances, it has been estimated that about one half of the area's acid rain has origins in emissions in the USA. The problem is bad in Europe too. It has been estimated that emissions from the UK account for some 5% of Sweden's sulphurous deposits and about 10% over Norway. The problem persists although the European Union has recently issued a directive to member states regarding the reductions in atmospheric pollutants that they must reach by 2010. These are sulphur dioxides, nitrous oxides, volatile organic compounds and ammonia. Each state has a set ceiling that it must not exceed by that year. This will not solve the problem of acid deposition across Europe, but is certainly a major step in the right direction.

HAZARDOUS WEATHER

In many parts of the world, weather can be a serious natural hazard. Its impact may be short-lived – from the disastrous transit of a tornado, to the devastating passage of severe gales lasting a day or so – or much more extensive, such as widespread flooding that may persist for weeks, or drought that may last for a season or longer.

The impact of hazardous weather can depend upon the economic health of the region or country affected. Inevitably, developing areas with poor infrastructure are hit far harder by events like hurricanes and drought. In developed countries, hazardous weather can have expensive consequences, especially for insurance companies concerned with risk assessment. Throughout the world, population and wealth tend to be concentrated in cities that are frequently in high-risk areas – by the coast, for example. In addition, modern urban complexes are probably more susceptible to hazardous conditions than they were in the past. The predicted changes associated with global warming include the possibility that intense frontal storms in middle latitudes will become more frequent, while the inexorable rise in global sea levels will lead to an increased flood risk in popular coastal areas.

The range of weather-related dangers in the USA alone is demonstrated by the record of disasters in 1995. The average annual number of deaths caused by weather events there between 1986 and 1995 was 485. In 1995, the total was 1364; the list below is not exhaustive.

HAZARDOUS WEATHER IN USA (1995)		
Event	Deaths	Damage (US$millions)
Lightning	85	33.1
Tornado	30	410.8
Thunderstorm winds	38	745.1
Hail	2	1,449.3
Cold	22	633.4
Heat	1021	456.9
Flash flood	60	902.4
River flood	20	348.1
Hurricanes/tropical storms	17	5,932.3
Snow/blizzard	11	108.5
High winds	46	121.0

A detailed examination of these figures reveals that there were 948 deaths in July followed by 171 in August.

Hazardous weather doesn't need to be as spectacular as a tornado or flood to cause large number of deaths. A good deal of these summer fatalities occurred in Illinois, where 629 died during an extreme heatwave between July 11 and 27.

Many people died in Chicago, and in Milwaukee, Wisconsin, where the state total was 89. Pennsylvania had 104 deaths. Of these deaths, 89% occurred in solidly-built homes, and 67% of those who succumbed were in the 60–89 year age range. This group is very vulnerable, as are the very young. In 1998, many older people also died in Texas and Oklahoma during the persistent extreme heat of summer.

TROPICAL STORMS AND HURRICANES

'Hurricane', 'typhoon' and 'cyclone' are some of the names used regionally to describe the same feature – a tropical revolving storm that is typically 500–800 km (300–500 mi) across, which has a ten-minute averaged surface wind speed of 64 knots. A tropical storm has winds between 34 and 64 knots, and is given a name or a number depending on the ocean basin over which it originated. The term 'hurricane' comes from the Spanish *huracan* and Portuguese *huracao*, which are also believed to originate from the Carib word *urican*, meaning 'big wind'. Similarly, typhoon is believed to originate from a Chinese dialect term *tai feng*, again meaning 'big wind'.

These extremely hazardous weather systems occur most commonly across the low-latitude northwest Pacific and its 'downstream' land areas, where just over a third of the global total of such storms develop. The northeast Pacific averages 17% of the world total, while the North Atlantic typically sees 12%. Of the remainder, around 12% affect Australia and surrounding areas (even North Island, New Zealand very

▼ *Cut-out view* of the central features of a hurricane. A hurricane is typically 500 to 800 km (300 to 500 mi) across and 15 km (10 mi) deep.

500 km
(300 mi)

15 km
(9 mi)

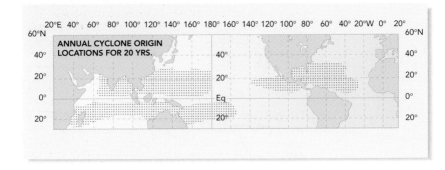

20°E 40° 60° 80° 100° 120° 140° 160° 180° 160° 140° 120° 100° 80° 60° 40° 20°W 0° 20°

ANNUAL CYCLONE ORIGIN LOCATIONS FOR 20 YRS.

occasionally), some 10% are found across the North Indian Ocean and about 7% occur over the South Indian and South Pacific Oceans.

The busiest time for tropical cyclones in the northern hemisphere is between July and October, with a peak during August and September, partly because the sea surface temperatures are at their highest then. This feeds more water vapour into the weather systems through evaporation. Similarly, in the southern hemisphere, the peak season occurs when the sea is warmest, in January and February.

▲ Tropical cyclone origins during a 20-year period. About 30% of all such storms originate in the northwest Pacific region.

A storm is born

As mentioned above, the temperature of the sea surface is critical for the birth of hurricanes, typhoons and the like. In fact, it must be warmer than about 27°C (81°F) down to a depth of some 60 m (200 ft). It isn't the sole criterion however, otherwise we might expect to see hurricanes popping up very frequently across tropical waters that are warmer than this all year round.

There are some more critical factors that have to be present before such storms can develop. Firstly the atmosphere must be in a state that promotes the growth of convective cloud through the depth of the troposphere. Additionally, the layer of air between about 3 to 6 km (2 to 4 mi) up must be reasonably humid so that the growing clouds are not eroded by dry air.

The growing clouds that compose the initial disturbance can only 'organise' in an environment where the wind speed does not change much with height – as is the case between the lower and upper troposphere. If there is a large difference in speed then the nascent disturbance is effectively 'blown apart', and development of the storm is halted.

The storm's structure

At the top of a hurricane, the air spirals out, in direct contrast to the inward swirling air in the lowest few kilometres (miles) of the troposphere. The strength and depth of this outflow play a crucial role in determining whether the system will become more vigorous or weaken. If the mass of air being thrown out in the highest reaches of a hurricane is greater than the rate at which it is being supplied in the lowest kilometre (mile) above the sea's surface, the surface pressure will fall and the winds will probably increase.

The centre of the hurricane storm system is known as the eye. It is typically 20–30 km (12–20 mi) across and experiences deeply subsiding air with generally cloud-free skies. Within the eye itself there is hardly any change of pressure across the surface. Very high winds occur where the horizontal pressure gradient is steep in the extreme, around the edge of the eye. Surrounding the eye is the eyewall cloud, which is like an upright cylinder and composed of extremely deep and vigorous cumulonimbus. It is across this zone that the worst winds and torrential rain occur.

Extremely strong winds and heavy rain will also be encountered elsewhere within the circulation of a hurricane, especially in the spiral rainbands that are also composed of very deep cumulonimbus. Although tropical cyclones are quite large features, many of the terrible conditions they produce are related to extremely deep thunderstorms embedded in their spiral rainbands and eyewall cloud. In effect, the large-scale pattern is made up from a significant number of smaller-scale cloud features.

The storm surge associated with a hurricane is caused by

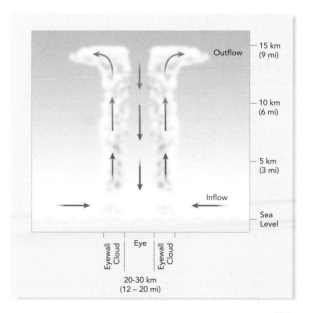

▶ *A vertical slice* **through** *the central features of a hurricane. At the top of a hurricane, air spirals out in direct contrast to the inward swirling air in the lowest few kilometres of the troposphere.*

151

the sea's surface becoming domed beneath a low-pressure system. In contrast, the surface is 'squashed' down by high pressure. This response of the sea's surface is called the inverse barometer effect, and for a 1 mbar change in air pressure, the sea level will rise or fall by roughly 1 cm (0.4 in). Thus, a very deep hurricane will be mirrored by a travelling region of elevated sea surface. To compound the impact of the surge, the hurricane's direction of motion adds to its height, as does the force of the wind on its forward right quadrant. The same applies on the forward left quadrant of such systems in the southern hemisphere.

▲ *Effect of barometric pressure* on the sea surface. High pressure 'squashes' the sea surface, low pressure causes the sea surface to rise. For this reason, a hurricane may be accompanied by an equally devastating storm surge.

Defining the strength

Although the traditional definition of the strength of a hurricane is Beaufort Force 12 ('air filled with foam, sea completely white with driving spray, visibility greatly reduced'), nowadays the Saffir-Simpson scale is also used, especially along the East and Gulf Coasts of the United States. This scale, ranging 1 to 5, refers to the magnitude of the average wind speed, the storm surge plus the nature of likely damage. It is used as a quick means of informing not only meteorologists, but also the public, of the relative intensity of an approaching storm.

The damage associated with the rare Category 5 hurricanes is tremendously costly, in both economic and social terms. It is defined as follows:

- Most trees and signs blown down.
- Very severe and extensive roof, window and door damage.
- Complete failure of roof structures on most homes and many industrial buildings.
- Some large buildings suffer complete structural failure, while some smaller ones are overturned and may be blown away.
- Complete destruction of mobile homes.
- Surge creates major damage to lower floors of all structures less than 5 m (16 ft) above mean-sea-level and within 450 m (1,500 ft) of the shore.
- Low-lying escape routes are cut by rising water three to five hours before the storm centre arrives.
- Evacuation of residential areas situated on low ground within 8–16 km (5–10 mi) of the shore may be required.

In the United States, deaths due to hurricanes have declined in recent decades because of improved forecasting and better levels of preparation for disaster. However, increasing coastal development from Texas to Maine is ensuring that there is a constant rise in the number of people who are vulnerable to the winds, torrential rain and coastal inundation from the surge that accompanies a hurricane. Florida's population, for example, has more than doubled to 14.6 million since 1970. Although fatalities have tumbled this century, the cost of the damage has increased significantly.

Typhoons are also the most costly and the most deadly natural disaster to affect Japan, South Korea, Taiwan, the Philippines and other coastal areas of South-East Asia. Across South-East Asia, the mean annual cost of damage over the period 1990 to 2000 was US$3.2 billion and the average number of fatalities 700.

Watches and warnings

The US National Weather Service regularly issues 'watches' and 'warnings' as a matter of routine, to alert the public to the risk of an impending serious weather hazard. A 'hurricane watch' means that a specific region faces the threat of hurricane conditions within 24–36 hours. It does not mean that evacuation will be necessary, but it implies that the population should be prepared for this if a 'warning' is issued. The latter occurs when severe weather has already been reported or is imminent, at which stage everyone in the vicinity should take the necessary precautions.

Typhoons and weaker tropical cyclones that affect the Western Pacific Ocean are monitored and predicted by the Joint Typhoon Warning Service based in Guam. They issue routine forecasts of a typhoon's intensity, location and track.

The costliest

The top ten costliest hurricanes for the United States since 1900 are shown in the table on page 153. Andrew was the most expensive natural disaster ever to strike the United States. It crossed the Bahamas as a category 4 hurricane

THE TOP TEN COSTLIEST HURRICANES IN USA			
		category	damage US$millions
Andrew	1992	4	26,500
Charley	2004	4	7,400
Hugo	1989	4	7,000
Floyd	1999	2	4,500
Fran	1996	3	3,200
Opal	1995	3	3,000
Georges	1998	2	2,310
Frederic	1979	3	2,300
Agnes	1972	1	2,100
Alicia	1983	3	2,000

before moving on to southern Florida. It produced a trail of damage over five days from 23 to 27 August 1992. Its eye moved onshore in Dade County – the central surface pressure of 922 mbar was the third lowest this century at landfall. The maximum sustained wind (averaged over 1 minute at a height of 10 m [30 ft]) was some 220 km/h (140mi/h) gusting to 265 km/h at landfall. It caused 15 deaths in the county and left about 250,000 people homeless.

Andrew took four hours to cross the Florida peninsula, during which time it weakened to a Category 1 hurricane. However, once free to move across the warm waters of the Gulf of Mexico, it regained most of its vigour and had a second, less devastating, landfall near Morgan City on the coast of Louisiana. It then moved north inland and was downgraded to a tropical storm within 10 hours.

Abandoned names

If a hurricane causes great damage, its name is never used again – so as not to tempt fate, perhaps. This is the case for David and Frederick (1979), Allen (1980), Alicia (1983), Elena and Gloria (1985), Gilbert and Joan (1988), Hugo (1989), Bob (1991), Andrew (1992) and Mitch (1998).

1998 – a busy North Atlantic season

The season was characterized by an inactive period that lasted until mid-August, when the start of the stream of weather disturbances occurred. Bonnie was the first of significance, running into the Bahamas before slowing and becoming stationary off the south-eastern shores of the United States. It moved slowly into the Carolinas, then headed north-east-wards to skirt the coast for many hundreds of kilometres.

Bonnie was followed by Charley, which attained the status of a tropical storm. The centre of this disturbance crossed the Texas coast near Corpus Christi to bring much-needed rainfall to many areas of drought-ridden central and southern Texas. However, people were drowned in and around Del Rio on the Rio Grande, where some 500 mm (20 in) of rain fell in the course of a day or two.

That summer was the first since 1892 that the North Atlantic experienced four hurricanes simultaneously. They were Georges, Ivan, Jeanne and Karl. Luckily, the last three roamed across the ocean without hitting land, although they did pose a threat to shipping. Ex–Karl ended up producing some wet and windy weather across parts of western Europe during late September. It is not uncommon for the remnants of hurricanes to rove that far, especially in late summer and early autumn.

Georges was another matter, however. On the backs of Bonnie, Danielle, Earl and Frances, all of which produced damage at various points along the US Atlantic seaboard and inland, Georges was the worst for fatalities. Georges rampaged through the Caribbean, with the Dominican Republic coming off worst; virtually all of the island's crops were destroyed. It struck north towards the Mississippi delta

▶ *Tropical storm tracks* over the North Atlantic in 1998. The summer of 1998 was the first since 1892 to experience four hurricanes

region, provoking the evacuation of some 1.5 million inhabitants from New Orleans and adjacent coastal areas. The city is around 2 m (7 ft) below sea level and is protected by huge levees and drainage channels built to withstand a Category 3 hurricane. Georges moved sluggishly towards the coast at about 9 km/h (6 mi/h), while its winds were roaring around its centre at approximately 160 km/h (100 mi/h). It produced some 200 mm (8 in) of rain at Pensacola, Florida, while other areas were predicted to receive over four times that amount.

The eye made landfall near Biloxi, Mississippi, with 165 km/h (104 mi/h) winds. 602 deaths were directly attributed to Georges across many Caribbean islands.

The 1998 season reached its tragic climax with the appearance of Hurricane Mitch in October. It was the strongest ever such system to be observed for the time of year: it formed on the 21 October about 580 km (365 mi) south of Jamaica. Early on 24 October, it had attained hurricane intensity and deepened rapidly to reach a minimum surface pressure estimated to be 905 mbar on 26 October. Its maximum sustained surface winds were thought to be near 285 km/h (180 mi/h) while offshore, but close to Honduras.

After moving around near the coast of Honduras for some time, it made landfall on the morning of 29 October then moved south across Honduras and Guatemala during the last two days of the month, producing

Type	Category	Line Colour
Depression	TD	
Tropical storm	TS	
Hurricane	1	
Hurricane	2	
Hurricane	3	
Hurricane	4	
Hurricane	5	

Tropical storm tracks — Year 1998

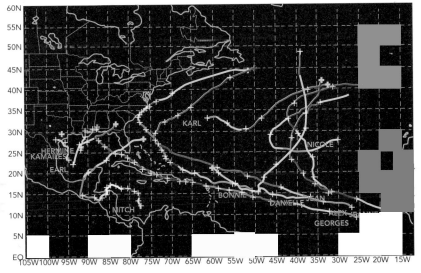

155

prolonged and extremely intense downpours as it did so. The devastating floods all but completely ruined the economies of those countries and caused around 11,000 fatalities. It is estimated that not since 1780 have so many people died in a hurricane disaster in the Caribbean/Gulf region.

Typhoon Maemi

Typhoon Maemi is fairly typical of powerful systems that hit South-East Asia. It developed as a weaker feature on 5 September 2003 and reached typhoon status two days later.

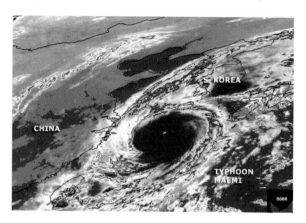

◀ *False colour image* of typhoon Maemi. Maemi formed as a tropical depression on Sept 5, 2003 in the Philippine Sea. It reached typhoon status by Sept 7, peaking on the 10th with maximum winds near 280 km/hr (150 knots or 170 mi/hr).

▼ *The storm track map* shows the path of typhoon Maemi. Maemi made landfall across southeast South Korea on Sept 12 with maximum winds near 195 km/hr (105 knots or 120 mi/hr).

It reached its maximum intensity on 10 September with one-minute average surface winds estimated at 150 knots. Maemi made landfall on South Korea on 12 September with torrential rains and battering winds of up to 105 knots. The system followed a typical curved path, embedded in the larger-scale flow.

South Korea suffered widespread flooding and landslips that left 117 dead, 25,000 homeless and damage estimated to be around US$4.1 billion. Its spiral rainbands and eye are clearly visible on the geostationary satellite image (above) that forecasters in the region would have used to help monitor its progress.

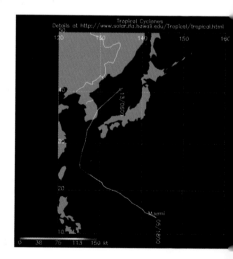

MONSOONS

The word monsoon comes from the Arabic 'mausam' meaning season. The essence of a monsoon climate is that, at the surface, there is a seasonal reversal

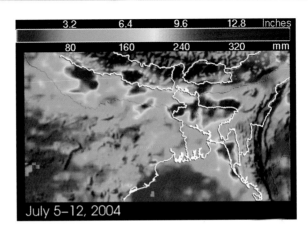

July 5–12, 2004

▶ *False-colour satellite image* of monsoon flooding over southern Asia, July 5–12 2004. Rainfall totals for the period 5–12 July 2004 are shown for southern Asia. Areas of 25 cm (10 in) or more (red areas) occur along southern Nepal, northern India and northern and southeastern Bangladesh. Some of the highest totals approaching 41 cm (16 in) (dark red areas) are over central Nepal and over the Khasi Hills near the border between province of Sylhet in Bangladesh and the state of Assam, India.

of the wind direction and associated wet and dry seasons. The best known monsoon is that across southern Asia – India in particular is well known for its monsoon season. There is a less well-known monsoon across West Africa, and the term is used to define seasonal changes across the south-western part of the USA.

Across the Indian subcontinent, low-level winds usually blow from the south-west during the wet summer monsoon and from the north-east over the period of the dry winter monsoon. Over India and surrounding countries, the summer rains are essential for the national well-being. The same is true across West Africa. Above average rainfall is of course welcome in dry climates except that it can occasionally cause significant problems, particularly over southern Asia.

The summer of 2002 proved to be below average in terms of the rainfall totals across India while 2003 was 6% above average. Interestingly, there is more than a suggestion that the summer monsoon 'success' may very well be related significantly to the occurrence of El Nino or La Nina (*see* pages 46–54). Both these occasional developments change the nature of the large-scale tropical atmospheric circulation in such a way that the former is associated with drier conditions and the latter with wetter ones. The south Asian monsoon of 2004 started some two weeks early across India and was some 21% above average for rainfall in June. However, the welcome rains proved fatal for many with 50 feared dead when a river burst its banks on 15 July and 30 perished as a boat capsized in eastern India on the same day.

By the third week of July the flooding was the worst for ten years in some parts, with about 10 million people displaced. A special meteorological satellite capable of mapping rainfall in the tropics illustrates the size of the wet anomalies across parts of southern Asia for a period of days in mid-July 2004.

SEVERE CONVECTION

'Severe convection' refers to troposphere-deep cumulus cloud that produces dangerous weather like lightning, hail, extreme gustiness and the occasional tornado. In the USA, a severe thunderstorm is defined as one that produces winds on the ground of at least 93 km/h (58 mi/h) and hailstones that are at least 20 mm (0.8 in) in diameter. Such a definition will be broadly the same in other countries where severe thunderstorms occur.

Hailstorms

It seems paradoxical that the largest hailstones (see pages 80–81) are observed during late spring/early summer. Although surface heating is intense, this is also the season when overrunning cold air at upper levels can lead to deep overturning motions within the troposphere, expressed by deep convection; water vapour concentrations are also high due to enhanced evaporation caused by the high surface temperatures. These conditions reach their height across the North American high plains, stretching from Texas to Alberta.

The number of hailstorms reported in the USA peaks in May and June, although April and July are also busy months. Damage to property ensues when hail reaches some 20 mm (0.8 in) in diameter – note that an average May and June will each experience over 2,000 storms that produce hail with a diameter larger than 50 mm (2 in)!

Many other parts of the world are affected by hailstorms; one city that has experienced seriously damaging events is Sydney in Australia. In mid and late April 1999 the city was hit twice by bad hailstorms. The first hit the southern suburbs, leaving a swathe of damage that cost many millions of dollars; hail the size of a man's fist crashed through tile roofs into peoples' living rooms. Just a few days later another severe storm ran across the city centre, producing hail up to the size of grapefruit that smashed tens of thousands of cars and again damaged roofs of some 20,000 domestic and industrial properties. At the time, it was the third most costly natural disaster in the nation's history after a cyclone in Darwin in 1974 and an earthquake that hit Newcastle, NSW in 1989. More recently north and north-west Sydney were hit by a storm on 25 October 2003. Very warm, moist air flowed off the sea from the east and north-east and was overrun by very much cooler air aloft. Very deep convective clouds developed in this environment, producing hailstones up to 5 or 6 cm (2 in) in diameter.

Other areas with hail problems include the wine producing area of Argentina, situated to the east of the Andes around Mendoza. Grape crops can be severely damaged by hail storms. Also, in early December 1997, 26 people died in Uttar

Hail

In the USA, hail causes about $100 million worth of damage every year, to both property and crops. The costliest hailstorm to date is one that occurred in Denver, Colorado, on 11 July 1990, when the damage totalled $625 million.

A Record Hailstone

The largest authenticated hailstone to fall in the USA was found at Coffeyville, Kansas, in September 1970. It weighed 757 grams (1.7lb) and had a diameter of some 14 cm (6 in)! A cross-section of this particular hailstone revealed the distinct layering within it.

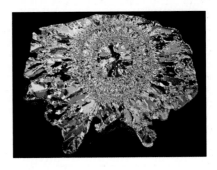

▶ *The Coffeyville hailstone in polarized light, illustrating a number of ice layers*

Pradesh in northeast India probably due to both large hail and lightning from the storm. Extensive damage to property and crops also occurred.

Downbursts

The intense precipitation that typifies the updraughts of mature thunderstorms evaporates as it falls, which can create an evaporatively chilled volume of air that descends from middle levels to the surface as a downdraught. When it reaches the surface, it flows out sideways as a 'density current' of cool, blustery air. If particularly intense and localized, it is known as a downburst or microburst depending on its width.

The sudden change of wind direction and speed as it spreads out across the surface is dangerous to aircraft that are landing or taking off, since aircraft must land and take off into the wind and all 'flaps' must be set properly. In the USA where severe convective clouds are particularly high risk in the spring and summer, all major airports are equipped with

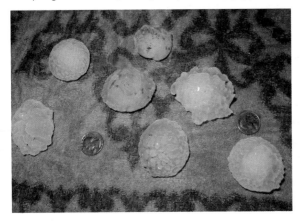

◀ *Large hailstones that fell over north St. Louis, Missouri, USA, April 10, 2001. Some hailstones measured up to 8 cm (3 in) across.*

Doppler radar to sense the location and approach of the threatening gustfronts. Short-term forecasts are issued to warn of the passage of these features across airports so that landing and taking-off operations can temporarily cease. Such potentially dangerous winds occur in many other areas too of course – in fact they can occur anywhere that thunderstorms are experienced.

Lightning

Lightning occurs very widely – by definition it must occur whenever there's a thunderstorm. In general, lightning is most frequent in tropical areas or where surface heating is marked enough to produce tall convective cloud.

The incidence of cloud-to-ground lightning flashes across the USA in 1991 displays a marked maximum in the humid, hot southeastern region of the country. Of course, there are flashes over the sea, but the vast majority are associated with deep convection over land. Florida had a notable maximum in 1991 with between 11 and 13 per square kilometre (third of a square mile) throughout the year, most of which would have occurred in the hotter months. In general, the higher incidences of lightning flash are confined to the region east of the Rockies, where warm, humid air from the Gulf is an important ingredient in the formation of thunderstorms.

In western USA, many fires, especially in forests, are started by lightning (see page 166). Over a decade, over 15,000 such fires occurred across the USA. These resulted in damage worth several hundred million dollars and the destruction of

▼ *Cloud to ground flash density* in 1991 *(flashes per km²). Florida and southeastern USA are the most frequently hit. Humid air from tropical waters is an important ingredient in the formation of thunderstorms.*

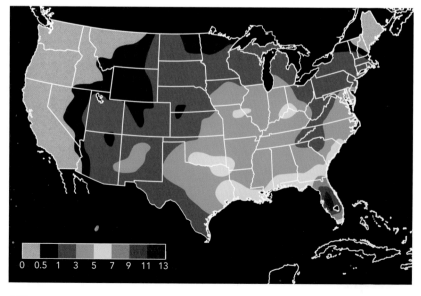

some two million acres of forest. In addition, on average, lightning causes 93 deaths and 300 injuries a year in the USA. Not surprisingly, drought conditions exacerbates the fire risk from lightning. This will be exemplified in the section on drought (see page 166).

Tornadoes

Tornadoes are always linked to a parent cumulonimbus cloud. Although many people confuse them with hurricanes, they are actually very much smaller. The most frequently observed size of a tornado's damage path is about 50 m wide with a track of 2–4 km (1–3 mi). However, the largest damage swathe can exceed 2 km (1 mi) in width, and the narrowest, 10 m (30 ft) or so. Tornadoes are most notorious in North America, but, with the exception of Antarctica, can occur in all other continents.

The US High Plains is the home of the notorious 'tornado alley' that stretches north from Texas towards the northern Plains states. This is where the most damaging offenders are most likely to occur. The basic reason that they occur preferentially in the area is related to its 'geography'. At the surface, much of Texas and Oklahoma, for example, can experience very warm and humid air on south-easterly flow that's come from the Gulf of Mexico. On the same day, to the west, there could very well be south-westerly flow that is hot and very dry, blowing in typically from New Mexico and northern Mexico. This baking air approaches the region at a higher level (because of the higher ground) than that from the Gulf – and overruns the warm, damp air. Where these two diverse streams converge is the 'dryline'.

At this point, we have south-easterlies at the lowest level, overrun by south-westerlies and the wind is therefore 'veering' with increasing height, or changing in a clockwise sense. Above, in the middle and higher troposphere, very much colder air should blow in from the northwest, across the Rocky Mountains.

These ingredients – the 'sticky' surface air layer that is capped by hot, dry air which in turn is topped with very much colder air are critical in stimulating deep convection. This can shoot up explosively as the daytime surface heating of the 'capped' moist layer progresses. Also of great importance is the way in which the wind veers with height, which adds a twist to massive storms that may develop.

Quite how, in detail, funnel clouds form is still a much-researched area. It is known, however, that sometimes shallow, elongated horizontal 'rolls' at the surface may be tilted into the vertical by some means – to be incorporated into massive thunderstorms. Such invisible rolling-pin like features may be the vestiges of old thunderstorm downdrafts, they could be lifted by the updraught that feeds a young but developing cumulus cloud.

A single tornado can last from a few seconds to over an hour. The typical duration is around five minutes. To be defined officially as a tornado, the vortex of rapidly spinning air must be in contact with the ground. This means that if debris is visible, even if there is no obvious funnel cloud, a tornado is present. The surface wind speeds are estimated from the nature of the damage produced – it is believed that they can reach up to 460 km/h (290mi/h) in the most extreme cases.

▲ *Tornado and base of parent* cumulonimbus *cloud photographed near Caldwell in Kansas, USA, on March 13, 1990. Tornadoes occur frequently from the southern US High Plains to the Dakotas and Great Lakes region.*

The cost
The worst American tornado for fatalities was the Tristate outbreak of 18 March 1925, when 689 people across Missouri, Illinois and Indiana lost their lives. It is a fact, however, that none of the top 25 US killer tornadoes have occurred since 1953, mainly as a result of improvements in forecasting and in conveying watches and warnings to the public.

The worst tornado outbreak ever to hit Oklahoma occurred on 3 May 1999. Tornadoes are well-known in the state, but this event was one of extreme severity, affecting heavily populated areas. More than 50 twisters ran across central Oklahoma that day; 40 people perished in, and to the southwest of, Oklahoma City. There were also outbreaks that day in parts of north Texas, eastern Oklahoma and south central Kansas. Five people died in Wichita.

One tornado in particular became the major killer, spawned by a massive supercell storm that had already produced a crop of tornadoes of up to F3 intensity in the countryside some distance to the southwest of Oklahoma City. A supercell is a massive rotating thunderstorm where the up- and down-draughts are more or less in balance such that the disturbance can persist for hours. This type of storm has a significant risk of producing tornadoes and damaging hail. It touched down close to the small town of Chickasha as an F1, then sped northeast menacingly towards the metropolitan region of Oklahoma City. On its way it geared up to F4 intensity,

The F-scale

The way in which tornado intensity is conveyed to the meteorologist and the public is by means of the Fujita (or F-) scale. This was devised by the meteorologist Theodore Fujita in the late 1960s and is set out below:

THE F SCALE		
F0	up to 115 km/h (71 mi/h)	light damage
F1	116 – 179 km/h (72–111 mi/h)	moderate damage
F2	180 – 251 km/h (112–156 mi/h)	considerable damage
F3	252 – 330 km/h (157–205 mi/h)	severe damage
F4	331 – 416 km/h (206–258 mi/h)	devastating damage
F5	over 417 km/h (259 mi/h)	incredible damage

declined to F3, then reintensified to a rare F5 tornado over the community of Bridge Creek where 680 homes were totally destroyed. A second, more destructive, 1.5 km-wide (1 mi) tornado grew near the Canadian River during the evening. It quickly attained F5 status and devastated Moore, a suburb of Oklahoma City. The destruction here was unbelievable; 1,225 houses and 274 apartments were razed along with 50 businesses, two schools and churches; 4,000 to 4,500 homes were also damaged. The estimated total cost bordered on US$1,000 million.

Predicting tornadoes

It will probably never be possible to predict the precise loca-tion and timing of a tornado, even one day ahead. Currently, forecasters in the USA can predict the risk of severe convec-tion one day ahead, and based on this knowledge, they issue advice for areas that may encompass a few US states, or regions within states, indicating an increased tornado risk.

The situation is monitored by routine surface observing stations (*see* pages 92–101), although they do not provide the fine detail of precipitation. Precipitation radars (*see* page 104) map the extent and intensity of rainfall, and indicate the location and movement of severe storms. However, such storms only register on this type of radar once they have started up. Doppler radar maps the regions of convergence and divergence in the lower atmosphere. Regions of convergence are the risk areas and are often useful precursors of deep convection.

Once severe storms develop, changes in motion and intensity can be monitored virtually continuously from the ground. Rapid scans (up to an image a minute) from the US geosynchronous weather satellites (see page 108) are permitted when conditions indicate a high risk of severe convection.

MID-LATITUDE FRONTAL STORMS

Europe never experiences true hurricanes. From time to time, mainly in the late summer and autumn, a system that began as a hurricane brings strong winds and heavy rain to western Europe. By the time it reaches these shores, however, its tropical characteristics will have died. Although winds may reach hurricane force on the Beaufort scale, they are produced by frontal depressions, not the systems that comprise of an eye and spiral rainbands that produce torrential rainfall. Significant strides have been made in improving the understanding of, and ability to predict, severe frontal systems that affect western Europe (or any geographically similar areas).

▼ *Radar rainfall map* for UK and Ireland, 00 UTC, January 25, 1990. The so-called Burns' Day Storm was just one component of Britain's wettest and warmest winter since 1914–15.

The Burns' Day Storm

Occasional severe weather warnings are issued in the UK every winter, often in relation to the passage of a deep frontal depression (very low central pressure) that can produce widespread wind damage and flooding. Sometimes, however, there may be an unusually extreme development of a rapidly deepening depression with winds of dangerous strength. The so-called Burns' Day Storm that rushed through the UK and Ireland on 25 January 1990 is one example.

The Burns' Day storm was only one component of this dramatic winter. It was the wettest and warmest in Britain since 1914–15. Across Scotland, for example, the three months from January to March 1990 each recorded a precipitation total that fell within the ten highest monthly values in Scotland since 1869. This period produced an average rainfall for Scotland of 791 mm (31 in) – the highest on record.

Groundwater levels for the UK in February 1990 had no modern precedent; run-off rates were enormous, and before the end of the first week of that month, most rivers were in spate. At Chilgrove Observation Borehole in West Sussex, the level rose by 40 m (130 ft) in eight weeks from a near-record low level in early December. In the western headwaters of the Tay, Britain's largest river in terms of discharge, 518 mm (20 in) were recorded in the 25 days leading up to 4 February. Moderate rainfall after the 4th, combined with substantial snowmelt in the mild weather, produced a peak flow at the Tay's Ballathie Gauging Station of 1,750 m³/sec (61,775 ft³/sec) – the highest rate ever recorded in the UK.

The depression and its attendant fronts were just approaching Ireland, Britain and France at midnight on 24 January, the warm front stretching from southwest Ireland, through the extreme west of Cornwall, to a point near Bordeaux, France. The radar network mapped the extent of the rain preceding the warm front as far ahead of the surface front as the southern Pennines and north Midlands.

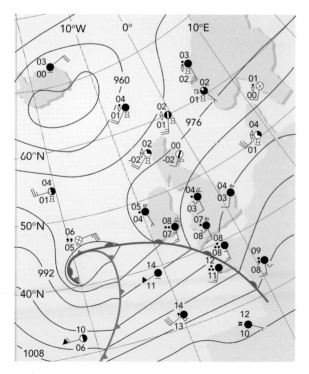

◄ **Surface weather map** for UK, 00 UTC, January 25, 1990. The Burn's Day Storm is a good example of a rapidly deepening frontal depression. Such depressions can bring very strong winds and the possibility of flooding.

165

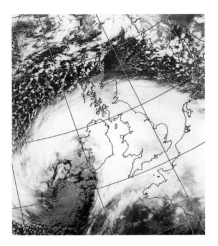

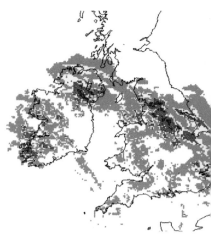

During the night, the system ran across the British Isles, and at 0329 UTC on 25 January, the forward edge of the warm front's cirrus was situated across the North Sea, while the cold front stretched away south-westwards from the Celtic Sea. By 0400 UTC, the rain had also moved on rapidly. By 1200 UTC, the centre of the low lay over northern England, and the frontal cloud mass had left most of the British Isles at the time of the satellite image at 1324 UTC. Much wind damage occurred across Britain. This included the widespread felling of many trees and some structural damage. As the storm swept across to the continent, it continued its destructive path over the Low Countries and Germany.

▲ *Satellite thermal infrared* image (0320 UTC) and radar rainfall map (0400 UTC), January 25, 1990. The rainfall map shows the northward progression of the worst rain in the four hours since the 0000 image (p165).

DROUGHT AND WILD FIRES

We are more aware nowadays that drought may be the result of atmospheric or oceanic anomalies that can be some distance from the suffering region. Recent work has indicated, for example, that higher than average sea surface temperature over parts of the Indian Ocean is probably related to the development of drought in the Sahel. This sub-Saharan region between about 10° and 20° North is renown for such stress. The evidence is that warmer tropical Indian Ocean waters (and to some extent tropical Atlantic ones too) produce deeper cumulus convection over the sea at the expense of weaker convergence over the African continent. This in turn means that precipitating cloud will be weaker/less frequent than average. The incidence of wild fires increases when drought conditions prevail.

Many regions of the world are susceptible to forest and bush fires, particularly those that experience a significant dry season during the year when conditions are hot. Some weather services advise forestry departments regarding the type of weather that increases the risk of such fires.

The occurrence of an El Niño (see pages 46–54) places tropical countries in the western Pacific region at a significantly higher risk than normal because of the enhanced, prolonged subsidence experienced there. Such subsidence is a characteristic of high pressure within which vast volumes of air sink gently towards the surface. The vast pollution event in Malaysia and Indonesia during September 1997, devastating bush fires during Australia in late 1997 and early 1998, and widespread forest fires in Borneo during April 1998 were all partly related to the 1997–98 El Niño.

Aussie bush fire

On 15 December 1997, Australian firefighters fought to control a massive bush fire in the northwest of the state of Victoria that had destroyed almost 4,000 hectares (9,900 acres) of natural scrub in the Murray-Sunset National Park. Some 45 fires had started on the previous day, due largely to lightning strikes. One fire co-ordinator stated that, 'With the number of fires for the current fire season exceeding those for the same period during the 1982–83 season, the indication is that we are in for a grim summer.' Interestingly, 1982–83 was the last time the world saw a strong El Niño.

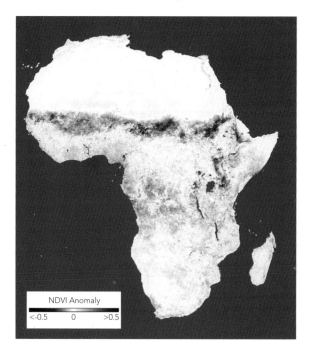

► *Multispectral image* of the African drought of 1984–85. Dark reddish-brown areas indicate unhealthy vegetation relative to a normal year. The drought withered crops from the Sahel (along the southern border of the Sahara desert) to East Africa and hit Ethiopia, Sudan and Somalia especially hard.

NDVI Anomaly

<-0.5   0   >0.5

During the period 3–9 January 1994, there were five days during which the 'McArthur Forest Fire Danger index' exceeded the value of 50, indicating extreme fire danger. The combination of circumstances that produced such 'ripe' conditions were a prolonged drought (a rain deficit of over 100 mm), a temperature of 35°C, a relative humidity of 15%, and a mean wind speed of 33 km/h (21 mi/h).

In January 1994, almost the whole of coastal New South Wales experienced weather that produced an extremely high risk of fire. Between 27 December 1993 and 16 January 1994, over 800 fires destroyed about 800,000 hectares (2,000,000 acres) of vegetation, and over 200 houses – mainly in suburban areas, including Sydney's. Two firefighters and two members of the public died due to the fires during this period. This loss was not as dramatic, however, as two other major events. On Ash Wednesday 1983, 76 people died and over 2,500 properties were burned down in the Adelaide Hills and outer Melbourne. Around Hobart, Tasmania, 62 died and over 1,300 buildings were destroyed in 1967. More recently, wildfires across many areas of Australia during 2002 and early 2003 – occurred during probably the worst drought since reliable records began in 1910. During the period from 1990 to 2001, it is estimated that about 11% of all natural disasters in Australia were drought-related. Indeed, the gross value of national farm production

▼ *Multichannel colour composite* image of *wildfires across southeast Australia, January 21, 2003. The 2002/2003 Summer season produced Australia's worst drought since records began.*

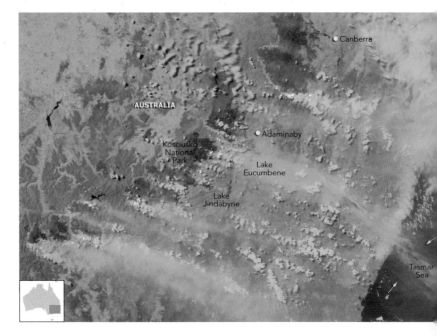

▶ **Rural firefighters** in Queensland, Australia tackle a blaze. Wildfires are a major problem in dry countries like Australia, however, controlled fire is also a very efficient tool for hazard reduction and can help to encourage pasture regrowth.

was about 20% down on average for the 2002/2003 period – a very significant drop.

Interestingly, there is a suspicion that since the temperature maxima recorded during the 2002 drought were the highest of any year since 1950 (and they were unusually warm compared to all five major droughts since then), the extreme heat may be a sign of global warming.

Just one of the many fires during the recent drought occurred in the Canberra region on 18 January 2003. A satellite's eye view of the fires, the scorched areas and the blowing smoke is illustrated in the above photo. On a local scale, the dense particulate matter produced by the fires is clear to see. Unfortunately, in the Canberra area four people perished and some 2,400 homes were destroyed.

An important message for town planners and local authorities is that these disasters will occur at regular intervals if urban development is permitted to encroach on surrounding forests and bushland. Despite this, development of this kind continues in southern California and parts of Australia.

HOLIDAY WEATHER

What we consider good holiday weather can vary from person to person. Most of us want dry conditions no matter where we are, the majority preferring warmth and sunshine, too. Those who enjoy outdoor pursuits such as mountain biking and windsurfing are not concerned about high temperatures. Light winds with good visibility and broken cloud may be more to their liking. This chapter gives general information on the duration of various aspects of the climate, at a variety of international holiday destinations.

Monthly average values of weather data illustrate the seasonal changes that make up part of an area's climate. The variations from month to month in average temperature, precipitation and sunshine are caused by the gradual evolution of the atmosphere's large-scale circulation patterns. The slow change in the intensity and location of the highs, lows and Intertropical Convergence Zone (ITCZ) (*see* pages 30–32) throughout the year control the nature and strength of the seasons at a particular site. When high pressure dominates, conditions will be dry, but they will be wet if low pressure, including the ITCZ, reigns.

The perception of a season depends partly on whether a location lies within or beyond the tropics (from about 30°N to 30°S). In the tropics, which experience only minor temperature changes throughout the year, seasons are marked by the presence or absence of rainfall. Outside the tropics, significant variation in the strength and duration of sunshine means that, in general, the seasons are defined on the basis of temperature change. There can be notable changes in precipitation, too.

Statements in this chapter about the duration of various aspects of the climate are quite broad in nature. The reason for this is that monthly values have been used rather than weekly, for example. The temperatures illustrated are average daily maxima and minima for a period of years. A given month's value – January, for example – is calculated by averaging that month's individual daily means of maximum and minimum temperature. If the location has a record of 30 years, the mean January values given are the averages of the 30 individual Januarys. What constitutes a rainy day varies from place to place, so the amount is usually quoted in the description. Where local sunshine totals or other variables are not readily available, those from sites with broadly similar characteristics have been used.

▼ *The Grand Canal in* ***Venice, Italy****. Venice has been a popular holiday destination for centuries. It has a climate similar to that of Florence (see page 176).*

EUROPE

Edinburgh, Scotland

The capital of Scotland typifies the relative dryness of the eastern side of Britain. Precipitation is on average lowest during February to April inclusive with a relatively wet period in the autumn. The maximum in July and August is mainly related to relatively short-lived convective systems.

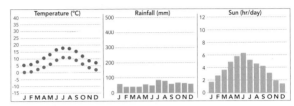

Bright sunshine hours are poor in the winter because of both the city's quite high latitude and the risk of dull conditions if the wind is coming off the North Sea – this is true of many British east coast locations throughout the year. May and June are the brightest months on average at a time when the high latitude is a definite advantage. The longer day-lengths in this period mean that occasionally, Scottish places can be sunnier than the Mediterranean.

Summer temperatures are comfortable, with a monthly average maximum of around 18°C (64°F) for July and August. Individual days within the summer can of course be warmer, particularly if the air flows up from the southwest or when anticyclonic flow approaches from across the Scottish mountains. Evenings in the summer are generally cool and can be decidedly chilly during the winter season when the monthly average minimum is around 1 to 2°C (34 to 36°F).

London, England

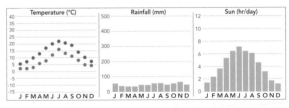

This characterizes the southeast of England, with a moderate annual range of temperature and, perhaps contrary to popular belief, quite moderate amounts of rain. The warmest months are July and August, which have only very marginally different mean temperatures. The hottest conditions in this area are associated with prolonged, cloud-free flow from a southerly quarter off the nearby continent, the more so if this flow

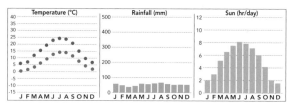

▲ *Tower Bridge, London, England.*
Sunshine hours and temperatures are highest in London from May to August.

has experienced a short sea track, which minimizes the cooling effect of the Channel on the air.

Snow is not very common in this large urban area and rarely settles. Rain is evenly distributed through the year and tends to be showery in the summer, in contrast to the more widespread frontal type during the autumn and winter. The annual fall of some 600 mm (24 in) is typical of low-lying southeast England as a whole. The number of days on which 0.25 mm or more falls varies from around one in two during the winter, to one in three in the summer. Sunshine hours are low in the short winter days, and are best during June, although the period from May to August sees over six hours a day on average.

Paris, France

Annual precipitation totals in the low-lying regions of northern France are quite sparse; Paris is no exception with an average fall of some 620 mm (24 in). Monthly values are well-spread through the year, with a tendency for a minimum during February to April inclusive and a minor peak during July and August when surface heating increases the risk of showers.

The annual range of temperature (the difference between the warmest and coldest months' mean temperature) illustrates that the city is rather more 'continental' than, for example, the French Channel ports to the northwest. This continentality generally increases with distance from the sea (*see* Prague, page 174, for example).

Summer days experience pleasant totals of bright sunshine, with an average of over 7 hours a day from May to August inclusive – temperatures in the high summer reach the mid-twenties on average. This is very pleasantly warm, although individual days can occasionally be much hotter. The average minima during summer indicate that such evenings are generally pleasant. The city's inland location means that its 'depth of winter' temperatures are comparable to those of Edinburgh in Scotland, quite some distance to the north.

▲ *Notre Dame and the Seine, Paris, France.*
Paris enjoys comfortable summer temperatures and winter temperatures rarely fall below freezing.

Berne, Switzerland

Berne's temperature range is relatively large as befits a city some distance from the sea. Summers are warm, while winters are cold, the period from mid-November to mid-March seeing an average minimum below 0°C (32°F).

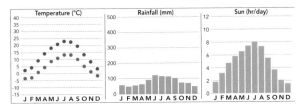

Much of the winter precipitation falls as snow, but the substantial seasonal maximum from May to September is usually rain associated with showery weather. This warm-season wetness is a common feature of continental interiors in middle and some higher latitudes. The pattern of rainy days, when 0.3 mm or more is observed, follows the same trend as the monthly totals. Sunshine totals are quite low in the depth of winter – generally two hours a day or less – while sunshine hours reach a peak from June to August. July is usually the sunniest month of the year, with an average of eight hours each day.

Prague, Czech Republic

The Czech capital records marginally over 500 mm (20 in) of precipitation in an average year with a marked seasonal inequality in its distribution. The months from October to March see typically around 30 mm (1.2 in) or less (much of this will fall as snow in the coldest months). In contrast, each month from May to August all record over twice that amount with a good deal of it falling as heavy, but relatively brief, showery rain.

The number of days on which a reasonable amount of rain/snow falls is typically one in five during winter or one in three during summer.

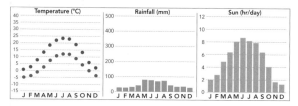

It is very cold in the winter, with January's mean maximum just managing to get above freezing (December and February are cold too, but not quite so much). Nights are very cold on average from November to March. Warmth picks up quickly in the spring and temperatures are very pleasant during the summer season.

The late spring and summer are also sunny, with over 8 hours of bright sunshine daily from May to August inclusive. The winter is fairly dull with less than 2 hours a day from November to January – broadly similar to Edinburgh and Paris (*see* pages 171 and 172).

St Petersburg, Russia

Although a coastal region, this part of northwest Russia is situated away from extensive areas of open sea. Therefore, it experiences quite a large annual range of temperature, from warm summer conditions – particularly when the air travels across the heated continent from a southerly quarter – to periods of intense winter cold under the influence of frigid air from either Eurasia, or the Arctic Ocean to the north. Winter is prolonged, the mean maximum only climbing above 0°C between April and November. As in many middle- and higher-latitude locations, the temperature rises rapidly in the spring and falls dramatically in the autumn.

Precipitation falls in the form of snow during the winter. It occurs typically on one out of two, or two out of three, days from November to March. The largest amounts of precipitation, however, are experienced during the summer and early autumn. In the warmer months, showery rain falls as the continent is heated, while the occasional frontal system produces much of the total in the autumn.

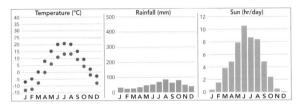

The monthly amount of sunshine varies greatly at this high latitude. Conditions in the depth of winter are bleak, with an average of less than one hour of sunshine a day during November, December and January. The best month for sun is June, with over ten hours a day, while May, July and August generally have more than eight hours.

Malaga, Spain

Another typical Mediterranean climate, but with a smaller annual temperature range than the more 'continental' eastern part of the basin. Malaga's average summer maximum is 2–3°C (3–5°F) lower than that of Athens, while the winter maximum is 3–4°C (5–7°F) higher.

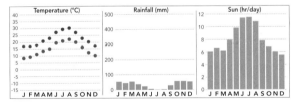

Malaga and southeast Spain generally experience a marked autumn and winter rainfall peak, which is associated with low-pressure systems that can be frontal (often moving in from the Atlantic) or 'cut-off' features. The latter are slow-moving, non-frontal low centres that can produce torrential rainfall. The number of days when 0.1 mm or more of rain falls ranges from an average of about one day in four, in the winter, to one or less a month in high summer. The higher total of rainy days experienced in the eastern Mediterranean region, exemplified by Athens (see pages 177–178), is due in part to the rain-bearing, low-pressure disturbances that actually form over the Mediterranean Sea and track eastwards. Sunshine is most plentiful from May to August, with marginally more sunshine in July. Even during the winter, the sunshine total is a respectable five or six hours a day. This means that a typical Malagan February is nearly as sunny as London in July.

Las Palmas, Canary Islands

These islands lie in a subtropical region that is dominated by the extensive Azores High (*see* page 26) as it intensifies and shifts northwards during the summer. Because the region is maritime, temperatures do not often reach uncomfortable extremes. Any really hot conditions are usually associated with a flow of air from the baking hot Sahara to the south-east, when summer temperatures can reach the mid- to high- 30s Celsius (high 80s Fahrenheit). In the main, winter temperatures are very comfortable, although cool air can sometimes sweep across the islands from the Atlantic to the north and northwest. Under such conditions, the minimum can fall to around 8°C (46°F) in extreme cases during December to March.

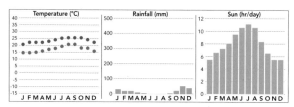

The area is very dry in the summer, particularly from May to September, during which an average of 20 mm (0.8 in) falls on five rainy days (those experiencing 0.1 mm or more). During October to March, the region is influenced more by mid-latitude disturbances, with an occasional frontal system or a slow-moving, low-pressure 'cut-off', the latter characterized by scattered heavy showers. Sunshine totals (for Santa Cruz de Tenerife – broadly similar to Las Palmas) are highest from May to August, with a peak of 11 hours a day on average in July. The duration during the winter season is typically five or six hours.

Florence, Italy

Florence illustrates classic Mediterranean climatic characteristics. The period from May to September all have warm or hot maxima (July and August are both over 30°C, 86°F on average) while the winter season is mild. No cool season month has a mean maximum below 10°C (50°F), although the winter nights can be chilly.

Its annual rainfall total is some 50% above that of Edinburgh's or Paris' for example – at around 900 mm (35 in). Florence has a typically Mediterranean seasonal distribution, such that June and July are the driest months with rain falling

▲ *River Arno, Florence, Italy*. *Florence has a typically Mediterranean climate with warm to hot summers and a mild winter.*

on one day in 5 to 8. The falls during spring and summer are most likely to be short-lived showers. However, October to December is a wet period, with substantial average falls that accumulate during the period when precipitation occurs on one day in 3 or 4.

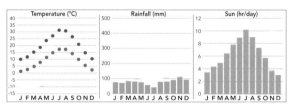

The area is most sunny during May to September as the Mediterranean region falls under the influence of the sub-tropical high. June to August are best, while the winter months see reasonable values of bright sun compared to locations further north in Europe, like Prague, for example (*see* page 174).

Athens, Greece

This location experiences a typical Mediterranean climate with hot, dry summers and mild, relatively wet winters. The hottest conditions are caused by outbreaks of intensely hot air from the Sahara. Maximum temperatures in the low 40s Celsius (100s Fahrenheit) are not unknown during high summer. Greece can suffer invasions of cold air from a northern quarter during the winter; in fact, in Athens, air frosts have been

recorded on rare occasions between November and April. The northern part of Greece is more prone to the cold air than the islands.

Rainfall is reasonably plentiful during the autumn and winter; indeed, on average, Athens is wetter than London in December and January. The same is not true of the summer, when Athens experiences very small amounts of rain from June to September. October is the month in the Mediterranean as a whole when the weather takes on a more disturbed state. The number of rainy days when 0.1 mm or more is observed varies from two or three a month, in high summer, to one day in two during December and February. Sunshine totals are at their best – more than ten hours a day – from June to the end of August.

▲ *The Erechtheion,* **situated on the** **Acropolis,** *Athens, Greece. Athens' mainland position puts it at risk from hot Saharan air.*

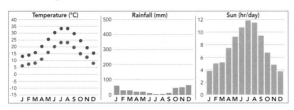

NORTH AMERICA

Vancouver, Canada

Vancouver is situated on the west coast of a continent in middle latitudes, this means that the city has a relatively high precipitation total (about 1.2 m [472 in] in an average year) and exhibits a marked wintertime maximum and summer minimum. The period from June to September is relatively dry – with the driest period in July and August.

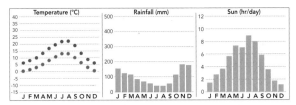

In contrast, every month from October to March inclusive records an average of over 100 mm (4 in), when precipitation occurs on some 50 to 60% of days. This is associated with northeast Pacific frontal depressions that influence the coast from Alaska to the Pacific northwest of the USA.

Vancouver's summer months are pleasantly warm and winter days generally cool. Bright sunshine hours are high from May to August, and particularly high in June and July. Predictably, considering the city's location, the winter months are dull with few sunshine hours. Many travelling, cloud-laden lows run into the region in the same way as western European shores are affected. Indeed, Vancouver is generally affected by maritime air – with lows in the winter from the ocean and air that has tracked around the North Pacific high in the summer (see pages 30–31).

Montreal, Canada

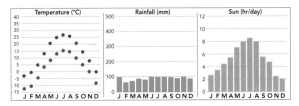

Montreal has a continental climate with very warm summer days and frigidly cold conditions during the winter. A glimpse at the summer and winter maps on pages 30 to 31 offers a reason for this. Eastern Canada is influenced by very cold continental air in the winter, when the approximate mean wind direction is northwesterly, bringing air from the freezing Canadian interior. In marked contrast, the general direction of the flow during summer is southerly, with air that has flowed to the region from subtropical areas.

From December to February monthly average maxima are well below freezing and the average monthly minima are below 0°C (32°F) from November to April. The warm summer

◄ *Montreal, Canada.*
Montreal has wide
seasonal variations with
very warm summers
and very cold winters.

means that there is a very sharp increase of mean temperature from March to May and similarly rapid decline from September to November.

Precipitation totals are high in every month, with a weak minimum in February and March. Snow is generally the principal form of precipitation from late autumn to early spring, with convective rain taking over in the warm season. Summer months have a risk of seeing precipitation on about 40% of days and the winter during some 50 to 60%.

Bright sunshine totals are over 7 hours a day from May to September inclusive while winter months are relatively bright with 2 to 3 hours a day.

Boston, Massachusetts, USA

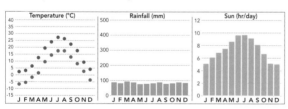

Although it is a coastal site, Boston – and most of the northeast coastal area of the USA – experiences a large annual range of temperature, peaking in the warmest months of June to August and dropping often dramatically from December to March. The warm summer temperatures are associated with the common flow of warm and very moist air from the southwest in the summer, around the western flank of the Azores High. The cold winter temperatures are caused by the outbreak of cold air from the high pressure that normally occurs across the interior of North America during the winter.

Precipitation is well distributed throughout the year, each month averaging a value between 79 mm (3.8 in) in May and

97 mm (3.1 in) in March. The number of days when more than 1 mm of precipitation (or about 10 mm [0.4 in] snow) falls ranges from six in October to nine in the following five months. The risk of snow is highest during December to February. Boston enjoys the sunniest conditions between May and August.

San Francisco, California, USA

For its latitude, the central Californian coast is quite cool, but temperatures are very much higher not far inland, away from the influence of the coastal fog and stratus cloud. Temperatures near the coast reach their highest during the late summer and early autumn. The winter is relatively mild.

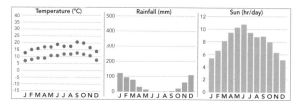

The thermal conditions in this region are strongly, but indirectly, influenced by the cool California Current, which flows south (towards the equator) along the coast. Moist air blown over this water is often cooled sufficiently to reach its dew-point temperature – the classic sea, or advection, fogs that lap over the Golden Gate Bridge are expressions of this. Apart from the fog, stratus cloud is also common along the coast. During the warmer months, it burns off so that just a little inland, temperatures become significantly higher.

▼ *Golden Gate Bridge, San Francisco, USA.*
The bay area is famous for the advection fog that occasionally shrouds the bridge.

Rainfall is quite strongly seasonal, indicating the dominance of oceanic high pressure in the summer and travelling frontal depressions during the winter. In that sense, San Francisco's rainfall regime is similar to a Mediterranean climate. The dry season of three or fewer rainy days a month (when more than 1 mm falls) runs from May to October inclusive; July and August are commonly completely dry. The wet season stretches from around November to March, when all months experience substantial totals from falls that typically occur on one day in three or four. The sunshine totals reach their highest in May and June, although the period from April to September sees average daily durations of nine hours or more.

Miami, Florida, USA

Not surprisingly, its near-tropical latitude means that Miami benefits from year-round warmth with very pleasant temperatures in the slightly cooler winter and monthly mean maxima that exceed 29°C (84°F) from May to October inclusive. Elevated minima during this period mean that nights are very warm – they are more comfortable during the winter.

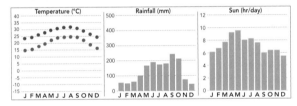

Rainfall is unevenly spread through the year with September and October seeing the highest totals on average – both with over 200 mm (8 in). June to August is also very wet. This whole period is when tropical disturbances are most active – mainly approaching the area from their genesis in the Trade Winds further south and east of southern Florida. The occasional tropical storm or hurricane can batter the region – with the greatest risk from around mid-August through early autumn. There is a pronounced dry period from around December to March when such disturbances do not occur and rain falls on only 15 to 20% of days compared to some 40 to 50% during the hottest months.

Sunshine totals are good all year round, although they peak (above 8 hours a day) from April to July and then slide to a short-term minimum in September that is related to the aforementioned cloud-bearing tropical disturbances. The other minimum occurs during December and January, although totals are still around 6 hours a day.

Aspen, Colorado, USA

Sites in the high Colorado Rockies are continental in terms of their large annual temperature range. Aspen's summer monthly mean maxima are pleasantly warm with values in the low to mid-twenties from May to August; nights can be cool however. The coldest months are December, January and February with low daytime maximum values (although still above freezing) but very cold nights. In fact, October to April inclusive all experience sub-zero mean minima.

Precipitation is principally in the form of snow during the coldest half of the year with a tendency for springtime and autumnal maxima. Broadly, the summertime is driest with the lowest falls (of rain) occurring from June to September, mainly as showers.

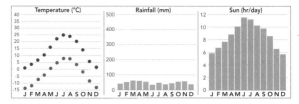

Although the 'driest', these months see rain on about 30% of days compared to about 20% of days in the winter.

The area is good for sunshine, even in winter when totals are broadly similar to Miami's, for example. During the period from April to September they compare very favourably to most other parts of the USA, reaching more than 10 hours a day during the high summer.

CARIBBEAN

Barbados, Windward Islands

Barbados is a maritime site, and is broadly representative of many of the Lesser Antillean islands. The region is influenced year-round by the Trade Winds of the tropical North Atlantic, which tend to have more cloudy disturbances embedded within them when the sea temperature is warmest.

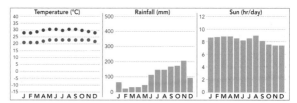

The annual range of temperature is typically very low: the warmest months see up to 31°C (88°F), while the coolest still experience a very warm 28°C (82°F). Like many tropical sites, Barbados' seasonality is based on the strong pattern of rainfall that develops during the year. Thus, the drier period dominates the months of February and March. It is during this time that rain (more than 0.25 mm) is seen on about one day in three, four or five. The wetter season peaks during September to November, when the total falls are high and typically occur on one day in two. Generally, except when the island experiences a slow-moving tropical cyclone, rainfall is intense and short-lived. Sunshine totals are reliably good all year round, although there is a tendency for slightly lower durations of sunshine through from September to December inclusive.

SOUTH AMERICA

Cancun, Mexico

This coastal resort in eastern Mexico experiences high temperatures all year round with a small annual range from the coolest (but still very warm) months of December to February and the hottest from June to September. Nights are warm or very warm throughout the year.

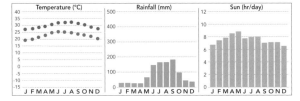

Rainfall totals reach an obvious peak from June to October with well over 100mm on average in each month. October is still fairly wet, although the number of 'rain days' is still only

◄ *El Castillo at Tulum,* an ancient Mayan site, overlooks the Caribbean near Cancun, Mexico. Cancun experiences high sunshine totals throughout the year.

about 1 in 6 compared to at least 1 in 2 during the wet season. The high totals are related to travelling tropical disturbances that generally come across the Caribbean to produce heavy, but not necessarily prolonged, rainfall. The driest period is from November to April.

Bright sunshine totals are good all year-round, with slightly lower values in December and January and the best durations from March to August.

Buenos Aires, Argentina

This city represents conditions in the low-lying region of central eastern Argentina and neighbouring Uruguay. It experiences quite a wide temperature range for a coastal site. This is because it is susceptible on the one hand to summertime outbreaks of stiflingly hot, humid air from Amazonia, and on the other to relatively cold air from the south-west and south in the winter. Very broadly, its temperature regime through the year is similar to that of the Mediterranean.

The number of rainy days (when more than 0.25 mm of rainfall occurs), is fairly constant throughout the year, with marginally higher frequencies from July to December, and generally lower frequencies during the remaining months. Rainfall totals vary to a greater extent – larger amounts being observed from October to December and during March and April. Drier conditions usually occur during the winter, from June to August. In the warm season, heavier rain often falls as intense bursts from deep cumulus clouds. During the winter, the rain tends to come more from the mid-latitude frontal depressions that track across the region from the direction of the Andes.

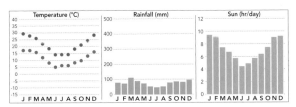

Sunshine hours are pleasantly high in the summer, but fall by around 50% during the winter months. Overall, the sunshine values are very similar to those experienced by countries in the Mediterranean.

AFRICA

Sousse, Tunisia

This location is typical of the African coast of the western Mediterranean, having hot, dry conditions in the summer months in association with the northward movement of the subtropical anticyclone. The deep, sinking motion of the high provides prolonged sunshine, high temperatures and arid conditions, which characterize summer in much of the Mediterranean region.

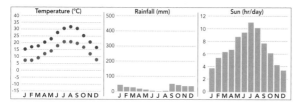

The marked increase in rainfall in the autumn and the persistence of fairly high totals (above 30–40 mm [1.2–1.6 in] a month) are linked to the passage of frontal depressions across the region. Sometimes, these penetrate from the Atlantic, otherwise they form over the warm Mediterranean or in the lee (east) of the Atlas Mountains.

Even the wetter months experience rain on only a few days; in fact, the number of days when more than 0.1 mm falls ranges from an average of one in July to a maximum of nine in December. This means that even in the wettest months, rain occurs on only one day in three or four. Sunshine totals from Annaba, some 250 km (155 mi) distant on the Algerian coast, indicate a maximum in July of 11 hours a day. Over eight hours of sunshine a day are experienced from around May to September, but this falls to four hours or so during November, December and January.

Cairo, Egypt

This location experiences a very arid desert climate typical of a large part of northeast Africa. Cairo's weather is dominated by the generally cloudless skies associated with the high pressure over the region. Heat is intense during the summer, the period from November to May is slightly cooler and therefore more comfortable. In the depth of winter, the minimum temperature can very occasionally fall to just above freezing in the cool desert nights.

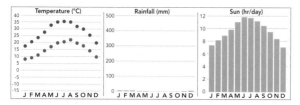

Rainfall is extremely low. More than 1 mm falls on only about six days in a typical year, and none at all is observed during June to August. The wettest months are December to March, with some 5 mm (0.2 in) each. A good deal of this rain is produced by cold fronts that track over this part of Africa from winter depressions running across the eastern Mediterranean. Not surprisingly, sunshine totals in one of the world's major deserts are high. There is a seasonal variation in the duration, from seven or eight hours in the cooler season, to over 11 hours a day from May to August.

Banjul, The Gambia

The small temperature variation between the warmest and coolest months in Banjul is fairly typical of a tropical location. The slight reduction in the maximum during July and August, which coincides with the higher minimum, is linked to the presence of cloud-laden and generally moist air from the winter (southern) hemisphere. This combination of cloud and moist air restricts daytime heating a little, while heat loss at night is suppressed.

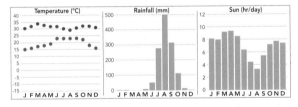

The ITCZ (see page 30–32) influences this part of West Africa during the height of the summer monsoon, with very large rainfall totals producing over 1 m (40 in) during July to September. During this period, measurable rain falls on slightly over one day in two. The single wet season is typical of a tropical location that lies at a latitude far enough from the equator to be influenced only once a year by the deep convective cloud and heavy rain of the ITCZ.

The quick decline to lower rainfall totals between the months of November and May, during which precipitation occurs on average on only three days, is a result of the establishment of an extensive continental high across North Africa. These months also experience the hottest conditions during the day, and the coolest at night – mainly because this area is frequently influenced by cloud-free (although often dust-laden), dry air blowing from the Sahara to the east. The generally clear skies promote heat loss at night, which is unlike the conditions experienced during the summer monsoon season.

Mombasa, Kenya

Mombasa is positioned close to the equator and therefore has a limited annual temperature range. The coolest conditions occur in July and August, when the Kenyan and adjacent countries' coasts are affected by air flowing northwards

across the equator, from the winter (southern) hemisphere towards the low centred over the Indian subcontinent. The warmest months of January to March are also the driest, with an occasional shower on one day in ten in February, and one in five in January and March.

Mombasa's location means that it experiences two wet seasons associated with the gradual southward passage of the ITCZ across the equator during October and November (rain on one day in three), and the northbound crossing from April to July (rain on one day in two). These are known as the 'short' and 'long' rains respectively. Sunshine values follow a pattern broadly related to that of rainfall. The totals are relatively high all year round, but the most prolonged sunshine tends to occur during the driest, least cloudy period, in February and March. The lowest durations (although still around 6.5–7.5 hours a day) are observed from April to June, during the major rainy season.

▲ *Mombasa, Kenya.*
Mombasa experiences high temperatures throughout the year, but has periods of dramatic rainfall during the rainy seasons.

Durban, South Africa

Durban and the south-eastern coastal stretches of South Africa experience similar temperature levels to those in the Mediterranean region. However, the similarity stops there: the warm season is also the wet season, as the area is influenced by heavy showers from disturbances that develop in the interior and the southwest Indian Ocean.

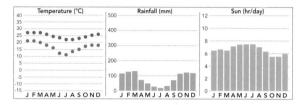

The warmest months are those of the southern summer, when the coastal areas can be influenced by very warm air from the interior. The driest period lasts from May to August, when an average of more than 1 mm of rain falls on only one day in ten and the region is influenced by the wintertime higher pressure of the interior. Because the warmest season is the wettest and, thus, the cloudiest, sunshine totals tend to be lowest then. The sunniest conditions normally occur from May to July.

▶ *Aerial View of* ***Durban*** *and Umhlanga Rocks, South Africa. Durban has a warm climate, the months of June to August experience the most rain.*

Cape Town, South Africa

Unlike Durban and the adjacent coastal area of South Africa, the Cape Town region has a Mediterranean-like climate. The summer is warm; the winter mild. Rainfall occurs on average during every month, but the main rainy season is the winter,

▲ **Table Mountain and Cape Town, South Africa.** *Cape Town enjoys a more Mediterranean-style climate that most of South Africa.*

when this region is strongly affected by the frontal depressions that sweep from west to east across the South Atlantic Ocean.

Usually, the wettest conditions are encountered from May to August, when the number of rainy days (those with 1 mm or more) is about one in three. This decreases to one day in ten or 15 between November and March. The area is generally quite sunny: totals in the summer are 10–11 hours a day, and in winter around six or more.

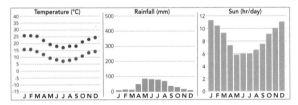

ASIA

Dubai, United Arab Emirates

This area is most pleasant temperature-wise during the winter and early spring with comfortable levels during the day and night. The days and nights become rapidly hotter from April to July, and conditions are still very warm during the downward trend in the autumn.

The winter season is when what rainfall occurs is most likely to happen and tends to come from the west or northwest along the Gulf. It can be showery and occasionally quite heavy, but statistics show that even in this period, rain occurs typically on only two days in the months of January, February and March. There is no rain at all during the period from July to October.

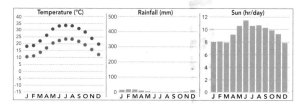

Sunshine totals are high throughout the year although slightly lower in winter when day length is shorter and there is some large-scale cloud. Duststorms can be a problem in the region during the dry season.

New Delhi, India

The Indian capital experiences a classic monsoon climate (*see* pages 156–157). Its month to month temperature pattern is unusual because of this, with the hottest conditions occurring in May, before the onset of the cooler (but still very warm) air that comes with the rains. The Delhi winter is pleasant with warm days and cool nights. Monthly mean maxima equal or exceed 30°C (86°F) from March to October however with very warm nights from May to September. Cooler air in the winter comes from the Asian anticyclone, which flow from a northerly quarter. Summer is characterised by winds from a southerly quarter, across the Indian Ocean.

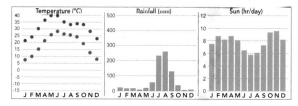

While the annual rainfall total is not immense at around 800 mm (31 in), a very large proportion of it falls during July, August and September. It doesn't rain every day during the summer monsoon, indeed reasonable rain amounts occur typically on one day in three in July and August. The period from October to May sees rain fall on one or two days per month.

The best period for bright sunshine is broadly from October to May with some 8 to 9 hours a day. This declines to around 6 a day during the rainy season.

Colombo, Sri Lanka

This island enjoys a classic low-latitude climate, with a very small annual range of temperature and double rainy seasons associated with the north and southward passages of the ITCZ. The hottest months tend to be in the late spring and early summer, before the cooler, cloudier air from the winter (southern) hemisphere penetrates the region as the summer monsoon sets in.

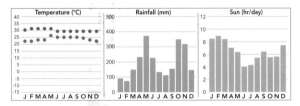

Rain occurs during every month of the year, although there is a strong double peak within the annual round. The first peak occurs from April to June, as the ITCZ moves slowly north toward India, and the second during October and November, as it crosses the island on its southbound migration. The great towering cumulonimbus clouds in this region of convergence produce short, but intense, rain showers. Sometimes the clouds merge to become larger-scale, longer-lived disturbances that generate prolonged heavy rain.

Colombo's annual fall of over 2 m (79 in) is fairly typical of a monsoon location at sea level. Rain falls on about two days in every three during the height of the ITCZ's presence, decreasing to about one in four or five days from January to March. This is when the region is most strongly affected by the less-disturbed flow coming from Asia in the winter.

Sunshine at a broadly similar location, Trivandrum, some 300 km (186 mi) to the northwest on the Indian coast, indicates that the best totals occur during the winter monsoon from December to March, when skies are often cloud-free. There is a fall in sunshine to a minimum at the very time of year when the potential is highest – in June. This is because of the frequent occurrence of cloud and rain in the summer monsoon. There is also a second decline during the southward passage of the ITCZ in October and November.

Phuket, Thailand

This site is typical of a low-latitude location near sea level, having persistently hot and humid conditions. The highest temperatures tend to occur, as with many other monsoon-influenced sites, before the onset of the rains associated with the migrating ITCZ. Thus, the slightly hotter period is normally during February, March and April. The number of rainy days increases sharply from only six in March to 19 in May, while the respective monthly average totals range from 74 mm (3 in) to 297 mm (12 in). There is a marginal decline in the rainfall around June, before the second, larger increase occurs during September and October. The dry season stretches from December to March. The driest weather of all occurs in January and February. Sunshine totals indicate that the best conditions occur from January to April, with upward of eight hours a day. Once the prolonged rainy season has set in, however, the duration falls to a little over five hours daily from September to November.

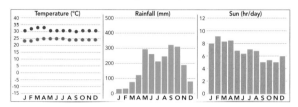

Hong Kong, China

This city lies in a region of Asia that is susceptible to cooler air from the Asian interior in winter. The highest temperatures occur during the wet season, when conditions are classically 'hot and steamy'. Such weather is most apparent from May to September, when the maxima and minima are elevated in conjunction with high rainfall totals due to the progress of the ITCZ across the region. Total rainfall is usually above 2 m (79 in) a year, which comes mostly in dramatic, intense bursts from tropical thunderstorms. There is a risk of even more

▼ *Hong Kong, China.*
Hong Kong experiences the majority of its rain between May and September.

dramatic amounts of rainfall over a day or two from typhoons. These are the cousins of hurricanes; in fact, they are the same kind of system with a different regional name. Like hurricanes, they grow out of features that begin as tropical depressions, then become tropical storms. They are most common in September on average but can occur during other months too.

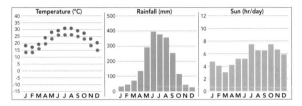

These tropical cyclones (large-scale low-pressure disturbances, ranging in intensity from depression to typhoon) are much more frequent in the northwest Pacific than any other tropical ocean region. In fact, some 33% of all the world's disturbances of this sort occur there, partly because the sea is unusually warm compared to the other ocean regions.

The height of the rainy summer monsoon season sees precipitation on one day in two, while the frequency during the dry winter monsoon season drops to between two and five days a month from November to February. During the latter period, the area is often dominated by the extensive Asian winter anticyclone. The occasional outbreak of cool air from this high can lead to air temperatures approaching 0°C (32°F) in extreme cases. Sunshine totals are best after the rainy season, when values typically reach a peak in October and November. The cloudiest conditions are usually experienced from February to April.

Tokyo, Japan

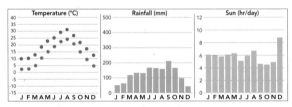

Although on the coast, Japan's capital experiences quite a large annual range of temperature. During winter, cool air often spills across the region from the high over Asia, with the coolest months from December to February. Daytime highs are however reasonable and nights can be chilly. In contrast, the summer is influenced by warm, moist air that streams up from a southerly quarter. Daytime highs are warm to hot from May to October – July and August are on average the most uncomfortable months with maxima around the high 20s to low 30s°C (80–90°F) and very warm nights.

The city sees about 1.4 m (5 in) of rain a year. Winter is driest by far, with air coming off the Asian continent; however, each month from March to October experiences over 100 mm 4 in) of rain as well as a risk of tropical disturbances. June to October is wettest of all, with tropical storms or typhoons an occasional threat to the city. During this time, rain can occur typically on one day in three or four while in winter it's one in five or six.

Bright sunshine totals vary through the year from best in December to poorest during the wettest fall months. Summertime values are moderate.

Denpasar, Bali, Indonesia

The Indonesian islands experience year-round warmth with very low seasonal variation in temperature. There is a tendency for July to September to be a little cooler during what is the dry season when rainfall is around 50 mm (2 in) or less per month. Monthly mean rainfall maxima and minima are slightly more elevated from October to May, with the rainy season (over 100 mm [4 in] a month) running from November to March inclusive.

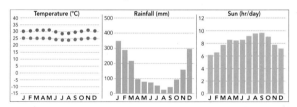

The largest falls occur during December to February when the Intertropical Convergence Zone (ITCZ) affects the area with its very deep convective cloud and thunderstorms. This area is near the Equator and therefore does not suffer typhoons or slightly weaker traveling lows. Denpasar is in southern Bali and is significantly wetter than the northern side of the island.

Sunshine totals are highest from around April until the year's end. The best values occur in the last third of the year and fall to around some six hours a day during the wet period at the start of the year. These sunshine values represent conditions some way removed from Bali, and are only a general guide.

INDIAN OCEAN

Port Victoria, Seychelles

This island group lies in the western Indian Ocean, at the same latitude as Kenya. The very small seasonal change in average temperatures is an expression of its oceanic location; the ranges are a mere 3°C (5°F) and 1°C (2°F) for the maxima and minima respectively. Extremely hot conditions are rare because the islands are relatively far from the continental sources of intensely heated air.

Rain falls during every month of the year, although it tends to take the form of very heavy showers. The driest months are typically July and August, when the ITCZ is at its northern-most point. During this period, rain falls on one day in four typically, and temperatures are slightly cooler, as the islands are influenced by the cross-equator monsoon flow from the southern hemisphere.

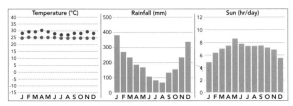

The wettest months of December and January see a total of some 700 mm (34 in) of rain, which accumulates in falls on one day in two. This is the time when the ITCZ has moved south into the southern summer and is most active in the region. The north-south migration of the ITCZ is much more apparent over the tropical continents than the oceans, because they are subjected to much broader changes in heating compared to the oceans. This means that low-latitude land locations often experience two main precipitation seasons in a year, whereas oceanic sites tend to see one prolonged precipitation period that peaks in one maximum because the ITCZ does not migrate so extensively over the tropical oceans.

Further south, toward Mauritius, Madagascar and Mozambique, there is a risk of intense cyclones (the regional name for hurricanes) when the sea's surface temperatures are at their height. December to February is the main risk period for these disturbances.

OCEANIA

Cairns, Queensland, Australia
Weatherwise, the northern part of Australia is a truly tropical region, and Cairns is no exception. There is a relatively small annual range of temperature between the warmest months of December to February and the cooler ones of June and July. Extremely high temperatures would be associated with a flow of bakingly hot summer air from the Australian interior to the southwest.

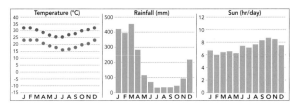

Temperature (°C)	Rainfall (mm)	Sun (hr/day)

As with many tropical locations, rainfall marks the seasonal change. Here, the wettest conditions occur during December to April, with very wet weather in January, February and March. This marked maximum is associated with the penetration of the ITCZ into parts of northern Australia during their summer season. Moreover, the Queensland coast – and northern Australia in general – is prone to tropical cyclones during the season of warmest sea temperatures. This is December to March in the southern hemisphere. The average number of days when about 0.25 mm or more rain falls ranges from about two in three during March, to one in four or so from June to October.

▼ *Sydney Opera House, Sydney, Australia. Sydney has high annual sunshine hours and warm to hot temperatures all year round.*

Sydney, New South Wales, Australia

The southeastern coastal sector and the southern fringe of Australia are, very broadly, similar to the Mediterranean in climate. Both regions are prone to very hot conditions from extensive deserts toward the equator, and to winter cold conditions that are ameliorated by tracts of sea toward the

poles. Sydney is protected from cold Antarctic blasts by the Southern Ocean, while North African coastal sites are similarly shielded from cold European air by the less-extensive, but warmer, Mediterranean Ocean.

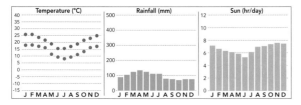

During the winter, this area experiences rain from frontal depressions that brush across southern Australia in the west-erlies of the Southern Ocean. Much of the southern coastal region of this continent has such a winter rainy spell. Rain falls during the summer, too, but more often in intense bursts from deep convective clouds. The number of days during which 0.25 mm or more is observed does not vary much during the year – from about one day in three in August to one day in two during January. Sunshine totals range from the highest during October to December, to the poorest between April and June.

Auckland, New Zealand

This area of New Zealand is essentially maritime, although it is not as conservative in its seasonal temperature variation as similar locations well within the tropics. The oceanic influ-ence has ensured that during a 100-year period, the highest temperature ever recorded was 32.2°C (90°F) in January and February, while the lowest was 0.6°C (33°F) in July. New Zealand is positioned far away from extensive continents that act as sources of hot air in the summer and cold in the winter. Any outbreaks of such air from Australia or Antarctica respectively are considerably ameliorated as they cross extensive oceans.

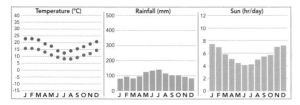

The warmest months are January and February, while the coolest is July. Sunshine totals are best from November to February, and generally poorest from May to July.

Fairly large falls of rain occur during most months, with a pronounced maximum during the winter, when many active frontal depressions sweep across New Zealand from the west. The four wettest months are May to August inclusive, when 0.25 mm or more falls during an average of two in three days. Tropical disturbances do influence this region in the summer and tend to produce heavy, more short-lived rainfall. Consequently, during the summer months, rain occurs typically on one day in three.

GLOSSARY

Absolute humidity Mass of water vapour contained in unit volume of air (including the water vapour)

Adiabatic cooling/warming Process of temperature change within ascending/descending air due to expansion/compression of the air. No heat is exchanged between the air and its 'environment'

Advection Transport rate of heat, moisture, etc. by motion of the atmosphere

Advection fog Fog produced by the cooling of damp air as it moves across a cooler surface

Aerosol Microscopic liquid and solid particles suspended in the atmosphere

Airmass An extensive area of air that has broadly similar temperature and humidity characteristics

Albedo The fraction of radiation reflected by a surface (usually expressed as a percentage)

Altocumulus Middle level cumulus cloud

Altostratus Middle level stratus cloud

Anemogram Paper strip chart used in an anemograph

Anemograph Instrument that charts a continuous trace of wind speed and direction

Anemometer Instrument for measuring wind speed

Aneroid barometer Instrument that measures atmospheric pressure

Anticyclone An extensive area of high pressure

Azores high Region of high pressure that often occurs across the subtropical North Atlantic

Back An anticlockwise change of wind direction over time

Barograph An instrument that measures atmospheric pressure and displays it as a time trace

Barometer An instrument that measures atmospheric pressure

Barometric pressure Another term for atmospheric pressure, as measured by a barometer

Beaufort Scale Means of assessing wind speed visually by relating it to how disturbed the sea surface is (or features of the land surface area)

Bergeron-Findeisen process Process in clouds whereby snowflakes grow at the expense of liquid water droplets where both are present

Blizzard A condition in which blowing snow seriously reduces surface visibility

Chloroflourocarbons (CFCs) Artificial chemical compounds that are powerful greenhouse gases and responsible for stratospheric ozone depletion

Cirrocumulus High cumulus cloud

Cirrostratus High stratus cloud

Cirrus High cloud with 'wispy' or 'striated' form

Cloud droplets Very small liquid droplets that compose cloud. Typically 0.02 mm diameter

Cloud street A line of shallow cumulus clouds that are generally non-precipitating, orientated with the wind shear between their base and top

Coalescence Process in clouds whereby droplets grow larger by 'bumping' into each other

Col A region of light wind on a surface pressure map that lies between two highs and two lows

Cold front The leading edge of cold air

Condensation Deposition of liquid water or ice from water vapour onto small nuclei within the atmosphere

Condensation nucleus Found in every cloud droplet or ice crystal; critical microscopic particle on which condensation occurs

Convergence The process whereby air flows towards a line or 'zone' from different directions

Conveyor belt Large-scale current that flows through a frontal depression

Cumulonimbus The deepest form of cumulus cloud, associated with precipitation, and thunder and lightning

Cumulus A 'heap' cloud that varies from a few hundred metres deep to troposphere deep

Cut-off A near-circular wind pattern in mid-latitudes and the subtropics; normally colder air that has been isolated or cut-off from very meandering higher latitude flow

Cyclone A travelling low pressure disturbance often associated with wind, cloud and precipitation

Depression A travelling low pressure disturbance usually associated with bad weather

Dew Deposition of liquid water droplets on the surface of the Earth by direct condensation from water vapour

Dewpoint temperature The temperature to which a sample of air must cool, at constant pressure and humidity mixing ratio, in order for saturation to occur

Diffuse radiation Part of solar radiation that comes from the sky, not directly from the solar 'disc'

Direct radiation Part of solar radiation that comes directly from the solar 'disc'

Divergence Process whereby the flow accelerates along its line of motion

Doppler radar Instrument used to map the component of air motion towards or away from itself, to spot low-level convergence/divergence, etc

Downdraught Localized, sudden and often strong gust of cool air within a shallow surface layer. Originates at higher levels within a deep convective cloud, flowing out at the surface

Drizzle Very small droplets of liquid precipitation with diameters between 0.2–0.5 mm

Dry adiabatic lapse rate Rate at which an unsaturated parcel of air cools/warms as it ascends/descends due to its expansion/compression. It is fixed at 9.8°C/ km

Dry bulb temperature Air temperature sensed by a mercury-in-glass thermometer

Dust storm Storm in which very large amounts of dust are raised upwards many hundreds of metres by strong winds. Occur mainly in hot deserts

El Niño Occasional relatively rapid warming of the sea surface locally around Peru during December, and/or widely across the equatorial Pacific

Ensemble method Forecasting technique which involves running many predictions in parallel, each of which has virtually the same initial conditions save a subtle change that varies from one forecast to the next.

ENSO (El Niño Southern Oscillation) Occasional large-scale air-sea interaction across the tropical Pacific, associated with even larger-scale climate anomalies over a year or so.

Environmental lapse rate Rate of change of temperature (and humidity) with height

Evaporation Process whereby liquid water changes to vapour

Evaporative cooling Process whereby air, for example, can be cooled by the evaporation of water drops held within, or falling through it

Eye Region at the centre of hurricanes, etc

Eyewall cloud 'Cylinder'-like region of cumulonimbus cloud and torrential rain that surrounds the eye in hurricanes, typhoons, etc

F-scale Scale that links the damage produced by tornadoes to their estimated wind speed

Ferrel cell The middle latitude cell in the vertical plane and north–south direction, with descent in the subtropics and ascent in the middle latitudes

Fog Horizontal visibility at the surface of less than 1,000 m due to suspended water droplets within the air

Front Leading edge of warm or cold air

Frontal depression Travelling low pressure disturbance with attendant warm, cold and, often, occluded fronts

Frost Condition of zero or sub-zero temperature often noted by icy deposit on grass, etc

Frostpoint The temperature at which air is saturated with respect to ice, by cooling at constant pressure and humidity mixing ratio

Funnel cloud Narrow snaking cloud that protrudes from the base of a parent cumulonimbus, associated with a tornado

Geostationary/geosynchronous Satellite orbit that is in phase with the speed of the Earth's rotation

Global warming The increase of global mean temperature believed to be associated with the artificial increase in greenhouse gas concentration

Graupel Ice particles from 2–5 mm in diameter, formed by accretion in some clouds

Greenhouse gas A gas that partly absorbs outgoing Earth radiation and re-emits part of it back down to act as a kind of 'insulator'

Gust front A line at the surface along which wind speed (and often direction) increases suddenly and strongly

Haboob Sand/dust storm in parts of Saharan Africa Hadley cell The tropical cell in the vertical plane and north–south direction, with deep ascent at low latitudes and subsidence in the subtropics

Haze Reduced horizontal visibility associated with high concentrations of very small suspended solid particles leading to a whitish appearance to the sky

Heat low A surface low pressure area generated over land/continental regions by intense heating

Heterosphere Layer of the atmosphere, above about 100 km, in which gases are layered/separated out

High Extensive area of relatively high pressure; can be slow-moving or mobile; associated with dry weather

Hill fog Fog caused by stratiform cloud intersecting hills

Hoar frost Icy deposits that form under generally calm, cloud-free conditions at night

Homosphere Region of the atmosphere in which the constituent gases (excluding water vapour) are well- mixed, and in virtually constant proportion

Humidity A measure of the water vapour content of air, expressed as relative humidity, absolute humidity, etc

Hurricane An intense cyclonic circulation that forms in the tropical North Atlantic and North-East Pacific

Hygrogram Strip chart produced by a hygrograph

Hygrometer Instrument measuring humidity of air

Hygrometric tables Tables that relate values of dry bulb, wet bulb and dewpoint temperature to each other, and to other humidity values

Ice fog Fog formed of ice crystals at low temperatures

Inversion A layer in the atmosphere within which temperature increases with height, at the surface on a clear, calm night, or above the tropopause, for example. Inversions of humidity also occur

Ionosphere Deep layer of the atmosphere above about 60 km in which the concentration of ions and free electrons reflects radio waves

Iridescence Patches of red and green, or sometimes blue and yellow, that occur on high clouds, most often within some 30 degrees of the Sun. Caused by the diffraction of sunlight by small cloud particles

Isobar Contour of constant mean-sea-level atmospheric pressure

Isotach Contour of constant wind speed

Isotherm Contour of constant temperature

Jetstream Well-defined zone of very strong winds

Kelvin Unit of temperature (K) with a base at absolute zero, such that 0C = 273K, 100C = 373K

Knot Unit used to express wind speed, one nautical mile per hour

Lapse rate The rate at which a variable changes with height in the atmosphere. A positive lapse rate means a decrease with increasing height.

Lee waves Waves in the troposphere often made visible by stationary lens-shaped clouds, to the lee of hills or mountains

Lenticular cloud Lens-shaped clouds that mark the presence of lee waves

Lightning Massive electrical discharge from cloud-to-cloud, cloud-to-ground or cloud-to-air, associated with thunderstorms

Long wave radiation Radiation emitted with relatively long wavelength (with respect to short wave solar radiation) by the Earth and atmosphere

Low An extensive area of relatively low pressure that is often mobile, but occasionally stationary

Maximum temperature The highest value of temperature recorded at one site over a fixed period of time, most commonly 24 hours

mbar Abbreviation for 'millibar' or one thousandth of a bar. Unit of pressure.

Mean-sea-level pressure Atmospheric pressure measured at a site has to be 'reduced' to mean-sea-level, which means that a 'correction' must be applied to the vast majority of barometric readings not taken at sea-level

Mercury barometer 'Official' means of measuring atmospheric pressure via the fluctuations in height of a mercury column

Mercury thermometer 'Official' means of measuring dry bulb and maximum temperature via the thermal expansion of mercury

Mesopause Upper boundary of the mesosphere at about 80 km above sea-level

Mesosphere Layer of the atmosphere above the stratosphere characterized by a decrease of temperature with height. Stretches from about 50 to 80 km above sea-level

Minimum temperature Lowest dry bulb temperature measured in a fixed time, e.g. 24 hours

Mist Reduced horizontal visibility greater than 1,000 m due to suspended water droplets

Monsoon Very large, sub-continental, scale reversal of surface wind direction on a seasonal basis

Nimbostratus Deep, precipitating stratiform cloud

Noctilucent cloud Thin bluish-white cloud around 80–90 km elevation, best viewed at twilight in polar and higher latitudes

Occluded front/occlusion Front with warm air lifted off the surface, cool or cold air at low levels, cloud and precipitation

Orographic cirrus High-level cloud occasionally formed by flow over a mountain/high hill roughly at right angles to the upper tropospheric flow

Orographic cloud Cloud formed by condensation within moist air flowing over hills or mountains

Ozone The tri-atomic form of oxygen

Ozone depletion The reduction of ozone concentration in the stratosphere due to the presence of artificial constituents

Pitot tube Narrow tube used to measure wind speed by sensing pressure imposed by airflow on the one open end; used on aircraft, for example

Polar cell Weak circulating cell in the vertical north–south plane, stretching from polar regions to higher middle latitudes

Polar orbiter Type of satellite orbit that crosses above polar regions on every orbit

Precipitation Solid and liquid particles that fall/settle within the atmosphere

Pressure Measure of the downward force per unit area at the Earth's surface exerted by the atmosphere above a point, often reduced to the datum of mean-sea-level. Also applies to a dynamic force on a vertical face due to the wind

Pressure tendency Rate of change of barometric pressure at a site, usually over three, six or 24 hours

Quasi-biennial Oscillation Reversal of wind direction in the equatorial lower stratosphere from westerly to easterly to westerly with an average 26 month period

Radiation fog Fog formed through strong cooling by radiative losses at the surface/lower atmosphere

Radiative warming/cooling The process of changing the temperature of air, for example, by the absorption (heating) or emission (cooling) of radiation

Radiometer Instrument that measures the intensity of infrared radiation emitted by a body

Radiosonde Balloon-borne instrument package that senses and relays data on dry bulb temperature, relative humidity, pressure and wind

Rainbow Optical phenomenon generated by refraction and internal reflection of sunlight shining onto a falling shower of raindrops, resulting in an arch of concentric coloured bands in a spectral sequence

Raingauge Instrument that measures equivalent depth of rain, as a total over a fixed period, or continuously

Relative humidity The ratio (expressed as a percentage) of the actual absolute humidity to the saturation value at the reported temperature

Ridge A region of high pressure that emanates from a larger anticyclone

Rime Frost formed by the deposition of super-cooled water drops under windy conditions

Roaring Forties Mid-latitude region of the Southern Ocean across which winds often reach gale-force

Rossby wave Large-scale 'long wave' in middle and upper troposphere in middle and higher latitudes

Saffir-Simpson scale Intensity scale relating surface wind speeds in hurricanes to their damage and surge height

Saturated adiabatic lapse rate Rate at which saturated air cools/warms due to expansion/ compression as it ascends/descends

Saturation State of a parcel of air that contains the maximum possible amount of water vapour for its temperature

Screen A white wooden box housing standard thermometers, etc, at a weather observing site

Scud Ragged low cloud that moves rapidly in the wind below a higher deck of rain cloud

Sea fog Fog formed by the passage of warm, moist air blowing across a cooler sea

Short wave radiation Relatively small wave-length radiation emitted by the Sun

Shower A short-lived, intense period of rain, hail or snow falling from a deep cumulus cloud

Snow Solid precipitation formed by the coagula-tion of ice crystals into various hexagonal shapes

Solar constant Magnitude of the constant flow of power from the Sun received at right angles to the solar beam at the top of the Earth's atmosphere equal to 1,376 watts per square metre

Solarimeter Instrument that measures the intensity of solar radiation

Southern Oscillation A 'see-saw' in mean-sea-level pressure; e.g. when the South-East Pacific High is weaker than average, the low to the north of Australia is shallower

Specific humidity Concentration of water vapour (gm) contained in a kilogram of air

Steam fog Shallow fog that forms as chilly air flows across much warmer water

Storm surge A positive departure in the eleva-tion of the sea surface produced by 'doming' underneath a travelling low pressure system

Stratiform General term for all layered cloud

Stratocumulus Low cloud that is sheet-like but composed of individual flattened 'lumpy' cells

Stratosphere Layer above the troposphere characterized by very stable conditions and dry air

Stratus Low cloud that has a featureless, flat base

Subcloud layer Zone between the surface and cloud base

Subsidence The process of sinking of air

Subtropical anticyclones Semi-permanent features of global weather and climate situated over the subtropical oceans

Supercooled cloud Cloud composed of liquid water droplets at a temperature below zero Celsius

Synoptic chart Map that depicts various weather elements at the surface or in the upper air at a specific time

Temperature Measure of the heat content of air

Thermal A plume of relatively warm air that ascends invisibly through a cooler environment

Thermal advection Change of temperature over time at one spot due to the horizontal movement of cold and warm airmasses

Thermocline Layer in the ocean through which temperature declines rapidly, separating the upper-ocean mixed layer from the cold, deep water

Thermogram Strip chart used in thermographs

Thermograph Instrument that produces a time trace of dry bulb temperature, often for one week

Thermosphere High region of the atmosphere above the mesopause within which temperature increases with height

Thunder Sound generated by intense and sudden heating of air by lightning

Thundercloud Deep convective cloud in the troposphere that is electrically active with lightning and therefore thunder

TIROS Television and Infrared Observation Satellite

Tornado Rapidly rotating, narrow, snaking column of air associated with a 'parent' cumu-lonimbus. It must reach the ground and is often made visible by a funnel cloud

Trades The North-East and South-East winds that blow across the tropical oceans, converging into the ITCZ

Tropical maritime Type of airmass with a source in subtropical anticyclones over the sea. Characterized in middle latitudes by mild, humid air in the warm sector of depressions

Tropical storm Particular stage of a tropical

cyclone when the system receives a name; category immediately below hurricane or equivalent

Tropopause 'Lid' that caps the troposphere, thin layer or surface where the temperature decrease with height ceases

Troposphere The lowest layer of the atmosphere characterized by deep overturning motion and virtually all weather. It is deepest at low latitudes and shallowest at high latitudes and typified by decreasing temperature with increasing height

Trough An elongated region of low pressure, often with a long axis along which there is a marked cyclonic wind shift

Turbosphere Deep layer of the Earth's atmosphere within which the gaseous components of the dry atmosphere are well mixed

Turbulence Small-scale (but can be larger-scale) random fluctuations of windspeed and direction

Typhoon Regional name for a tropical cyclone that has reached hurricane-equivalent intensity in the North-West Pacific

Ultraviolet Region of the electromagnetic spectrum with wavelengths shorter than the violet end of the visible spectrum

Updraught Upward-flowing air within cumulus clouds and invisible thermals. They vary from a few to many tens of metres per second

Vane A vertical, plate-like indicator that points into the wind to reveal its direction

Vapour pressure That part of barometric pressure exerted by the column total of water vapour above a point

Veer A clockwise change of wind direction with time at one place OR with height above one place at a given time

Virgae Lines of precipitation that appear from cloudbase but do not reach the surface

Visibility The minimum horizontal visibility observed at a site at a particular time

Visible radiation The range of wavelengths of radiation to which our eyes are attuned

Walker cell Large-scale cells in the vertical plane around the equator

Warm front The leading edge of the warm, moist air in a frontal depression. A gently sloping surface

Warm sector The region between the warm and cold fronts, generally cloud-laden, mild and moist air with occasional precipitation

Water vapour Invisible form of water in the atmosphere

Wet bulb temperature The temperature recorded by the wet bulb thermometer in a screen; that to which air cools by evaporating water into it until saturated (at constant pressure)

Wind Air in motion; speed measured by an anemometer

Windshear Change of wind direction and/or speed above a site at a given time or in the horizontal plane

Zonal mean Produced by averaging all values of, say, mean surface temperature for a month/season. etc, at all sites in a latitude strip to obtain one value

FURTHER READING

Ahrens, C. D., **Meteorology Today: An introduction to weather, climate and the environment.** *Cole, 7th Edition 2003*

Baker, K., **Be Your Own Weather Expert.** *Merlin, 1995*

Barry R. G. & Chorley, R. J., **Atmosphere, Weather and Climate.** *Routledge, 8th Edition 2003*

Bluestein, H., **Tornado Alley: monster storms of the Great Plains.** *Oxford, 1999*

Burroughs W. J. et al,. **Collins Weather, The ultimate guide to the elements.** *Harper Collins, 1996*

Burroughs, W.J., **Weather Cycles: real or imaginary?** *Cambridge, 2nd Edition, 2003*

Crowder, Bob, **The Wonders of the Weather.** *Australian Govt Pub, 1995*

Dunlop, S., Collins, **Gem Weather Photoguide.** *Harper Collins, 1996*

Eden, P., **Weatherwise.** *Macmillan, 1995*

Houghton, D., **Weather at Sea.** *Fernhurst, 2nd Edition 1998*

Houghton J. T. (Ed), **Climate Change 1995, The science of climate change.** *CUP, 1996*

McIlveen, R., **Fundamentals of weather and climate.** *Stanley Thornes, 1998*

Pedgley, D., **Mountain Weather.** *Cicerone Press, 2nd Edition 1997*

Reynolds, R., **Weather Rage.** *Taylor & Francis. 2003*

Stull, Roland, B., **Meteorology for Scientists and Engineers.** *Brooks/Cole, 2nd Edition 2000*

Williams, J., **The Weather Book.** *USA Today, 1992*

Useful Websites

American Meteorological Society
www.ametsoc.org

Australian Meteorological Society
www.amos.org.au

Canadian Meteorological Society
www.cmos.ca

European Centre for Medium-Range Weather Forecasts
www.ecmwf.int

European Meteorological Satellite Organization
www.eumetsat.de

Intergovernmental Panel on Climate Change
www.ipcc.ch

New Zealand Meteorological Society
http://metsoc.rsnz.org

Royal Meteorological Society
www.rmets.org

UK Meteorological Office
www.metoffice.gov.uk

World Meteorological Organization
www.wmo.ch

International Project to exchange schools' weather data
www.metlink.org

Using home computers to help run climate models
www.climateprediction.net

World climate data (and general link to other sites)
www.wunderground.com

CREDITS

INDEX